SEXUAL
POLITICS

D1520083

Series on Law, Politics, and Society

SEXUAL POLITICS

The Gay Person in America Today

SHANNON GILREATH

The University of Akron Press
Akron, Ohio

Copyright © 2006 Shannon Gilreath
All rights reserved
First edition 2006
Manufactured in the United States of America
10 09 08 07 06 5 4 3 2 1

All inquiries and permissions requests should be addressed to the publisher,
The University of Akron Press, Akron, OH 44325–1703

Library of Congress Cataloging-in-Publication Data

Gilreath, Shannon, 1977-
    Sexual politics : the gay person in America today / Shannon Gilreath.— 1st ed.
        p. cm. — (Series on law, politics, and society)
    Includes bibliographical references and index.
    ISBN-13: 978-1-931968-34-8 (cloth : alk. paper)
    ISBN-10: 1-931968-34-9 (cloth : alk. paper)
    1. Gays—United States—Social conditions. 2. Gay rights—United States.
    3. Homophobia—United States. I. Title. II. Series.
    HQ76.3.U5G55 2006
    306.76'60973—dc22   2006002269

The paper used in this publication meets the minimum requirements of American
National Standard for Information Sciences—Permanence of Paper for Printed Library
Materials, ANSI z39.48—1984. ∞

Cover design by Jordan McLaughlin.

These thoughts are dedicated
to Beau Ward and Shane Ward, who give me courage,
and to my many "out" sisters and brothers—you are my heroes.

A partial listing of those I know and love includes
Gus Chrysson
Max Wolff
Kevin Crutchfield
Mark Huffman
Will Shields
Chase Key
Miki Felsenburg
Daniel Bates
Robert Davidson
Gary Lowman
Monique Williams
Dan Ellison
Wil Nordbruch

But mostly these thoughts are dedicated to the generations of young people who will come of age in the twenty-first century. To these innocents falls the task of eradicating bigotry, promoting acceptance, challenging despotism, and achieving equality—in short—making possible the fuller enjoyment of "life, liberty, and the pursuit of happiness" for every person.

Contents

Appendix

Preface

The only true hope for civilization—the conviction of the individual that his inner life can affect outward events and that, whether or not he does so, he is responsible for them.

—Stephen Spender

IN 1906, W. E. B. DU BOIS OPINED that "the problem of the twentieth century will be the problem of the color line." In the fledgling years of the twenty-first century, I find myself wondering whether this century's problem won't be the sexuality line. An ominous shadow crept across the horizon of gay rights in the early morning hours of November 3, 2004, as it became apparent that John Kerry, the presidential candidate who, despite disavowing gay marriage, was the best political choice for American gays, was defeated, in no small part due to his refusal to distance himself from gays entirely.

If after the utterly homophobic performance by Pat Buchanan at the 1992 Republican National Convention, gays felt they were in, as Gregory King of the Human Rights Campaign put it, "the election of our lives," gays found themselves no less scrutinized, sexualized, or vilified in the 2004 campaign. The run-up to election day 2004 was marred by an ugly discussion of amending the federal Constitution to ban gay marriage and civil unions, and, indeed, several states did just that to their state constitutions. Election exit polling showed that "morality"—not two years of futile war in Iraq, government secrecy not seen since Nixon days, a tanked economy, or the ballooning deficit—was the single top issue cited by voters.

Those of us who had pinned many of our hopes for the future on Kerry's election (really more on the political climate that we hoped would emerge in a Bush-free nation) couldn't help but shudder, couldn't help but feel that somehow, cosmically, across time, the heavy foot of history had tamped upon our collective graves. Time will tell whether our concern over the election outcome is warranted—the progress of gay rights won't be derailed entirely, but surely our efforts have been hindered. The tide of conservatism and moral Calvinism that kept Bush in office also swept in eleven more state marriage amendments—Arkansas, Georgia, Kentucky, Michigan, Mississippi, Montana, North Dakota, Ohio, Oklahoma, Oregon, and Utah.

But, prior to the election, there was among many gay people an overriding apathy toward the American political process. Long before election day, I presided at a gathering of young gay men to discuss the proposed federal marriage amendment. I was surprised and chagrined to hear so many voices in this chorus offering an overwhelmingly defeated conception of their place in the American republic. More than once I heard, "Why should I get involved? Why should it matter who wins the election? Nobody will do anything for us anyway." These exchanges and many more like them were the genesis of this book. The results of November 2, 2004 simply cemented my conviction of its necessity. As Dr. Martin Luther King Jr. recorded in his 1967 book, *Where Do We Go from Here: Community or Chaos?*: "One of the great liabilities of history is that all too many people fail to remain awake through great periods of social change . . . fraternities of the indifferent who are notorious for sleeping through revolutions. But today our very survival depends on our ability to stay awake, to adjust to new ideas, to remain vigilant and to face the challenge of change."

Amen, I say, and *allons!* I hope that this book will challenge its reader to awaken to this revolution and to turn necessary attention to the politics that will bring the gay person the deserved equality that is so long overdue.

Acknowledgments

THIS IS A RELATIVELY SHORT BOOK that entails a relatively long list of thanks. First, I would like to thank the authors and scholars from whose work I have drawn in writing this book. Despite the logistical choice of limited citation (unheard of and uncomfortable for law scholars), I would like particularly to note the work of Arthur Lipkin, on which I drew heavily for the retrospective aspects of chapter 1, and that of Alan Dershowitz, Letha Scanzoni, Virginia Mollenkott, and Bruce Bawer, on which I particularly relied in chapter 2. I should also acknowledge that part of chapter 3 was published originally in the *Texas Journal on Civil Liberties and Civil Rights* as "The Technicolor Constitution: Popular Constitutionalism, Ethical Norms, and Legal Pedagogy," (volume 9, pages 23–44).

Many people saw the value of this project and encouraged me to turn my thoughts into a book. For comments on a previous draft, I thank Professors Michael Curtis, Wilson Parker, Michael Perry, Dick Schneider, Suzanne Reynolds, and Bryan Wildenthal. They, of course, cannot be held responsible for errors in opinion they tried to correct. I also thank Associate Deans Miles Foy and Marian Parker at Wake Forest University School of Law for facilitating research assistance and for other support. Thanks go to Scott Gerber for introducing me to the University of Akron Press and to Chris Banks, my editor there, a more dedicated champion and patient shepherd for this work I could not have hoped for. I also thank Amy Freels for her skillful and gracious production coordination. I thank Dean Bill Leonard of Wake Forest University Divinity School and Steve Nickles for initially encouraging me to teach my course on sexuality and the law.

I thank research assistant Gail Sullivan, particularly for her work compiling the information for the appendix, and graduate student Jarica Watts proved a most efficient and capable manuscript editor. Thanks also to Beth Malone and Ellen Makaravage for computing assistance.

Additional thanks go to Mr. and Mrs. F. for renewing my faith when it lagged, and to Dr. Maya Angelou for her inspiration to liberation through the written word. I must also express my gratitude to the "café crew": Kevin, Chase, Matthew, Daniel, Max, Gus, Monique, Katie, Greg, Jorge, Chris, and Brooke, who in general good humor put up with my frequent outbursts occasioned by writing this book.

Finally, but perhaps foremost really, I must thank the students of Wake Forest University (Divinity School, Women's and Gender Studies Program, and Law School) who participated in a dialogue about many of the issues that found their way into this book. Indeed, the missing ingredient in this book is just that kind of interactive dialogue. Perhaps I can make up a little for that by extending to the reader an invitation to share her or his thoughts. You may e-mail me at gilreasd@law.wfu.edu, and I will do my best to respond.

PART 1

Oh, I ran to the rock to hide my face.
The rock cried out, "No hiding place!"
No hiding place down here.

—Traditional

INTRODUCTION

For Jimmy

The very time I thought I was lost, My dungeon shook and my chains fell off.

—James Baldwin, *The Fire Next Time*

Amongst the many icons cluttering the walls of my home library is a photograph of James Baldwin. Baldwin has been my hero since I read with voracious interest *The Fire Next Time* many years ago. *The Fire Next Time*, a book that ignited blacks and whites alike in the other great civil rights struggle in our country, the struggle for African American equality, is, in my opinion, a work never equaled. Baldwin, also a gay man, wrote in contribution to the gay rights struggle as well, notably *Giovanni's Room*. But there is nothing like *The Fire Next Time*. It was something of a love letter to the American people; critical and chastening at times, it was, above all, loving and hopeful.

The love letter is an art little-practiced these days. In our instant-messaging, Internet world, few people know how to write a good one, and fewer still know how to receive one in the right spirit. This book, despite its weighty title, is my own love letter to my country, for I love it above all other countries. It is because of that very love that I reserve the right to criticize it—vehemently and frequently. Like the themes explored in these pages, the love letter is at once a private and a public thing: private in its intimate, sensitive topics and public in its commitment of such thoughts to paper and delivering them to the beloved. The love letter is an act of some courage, for it lays out things that are frightening because there is the possibility they will go unfulfilled, unrealized, unrecognized. Yet these things so terrific as to be otherwise unutterable must be uttered, because to do otherwise would be a horrible, untenable neglect.

These things must be spoken because gay people, on the whole, live lives of silent disillusionment, believing that their country and its politics have failed them. They ignore their inner urgings to action and swallow hard against the voice struggling to find its way into the open, because they believe that the voice will fall on deaf ears. What I hope for is a turning of some of these secret longings into public aspirations, worked for and toward as public realities. I hope for a gay community that approaches its country, mindful of its circumstances, with attention and care and with a broader, deeper politics of transformation than the gay community otherwise has practiced. This book is an invitation to turn essential attention to our neglected lives and needs and desires. My writing is nurtured by political commitment and the hope that writing of the kind represented here can make a difference in changing the rancor and discord of the gay rights debate into a conversation of reason and understanding.

I don't think it unfair of me to say that society in general does not know what to think about gay people. Generations of social taboos about sexuality, and homosexuality in particular, have left a void in the community's understanding. Recent times have seen enormous advances in filling that void. Slowly, slowly, the homosexual as a socially tolerable sexual variation has replaced the homosexual as a sexual invert. Despite the reactionary backlash that followed the U.S. Supreme Court's decision in *Lawrence v. Texas*, enormous strides have been made in the recognition of gays as valid, contributing members of our society, deserving of some measure of respect and legal protection. But gays remain unequal citizens. Even the gay rights movement has been scant on actual discourse about gays as people, as opposed to political or legal objects about whom much has been said in the way of rights and legalities but about whom very little has been said in terms of personal experience. Some of that has been a necessary consequence of policy arguments that have resulted in an increased measure of social tolerance for gays but have done little to advance true understanding. The gap between tolerance, which, in my opinion, is worth little more than the effort to say the word, and true understanding is very wide indeed.

This book is titled *Sexual Politics*. For some, no doubt, this is a curious concept. To the many Americans not engaged in the battle for gay rights, what happens in the bedroom (the sexual) is a matter completely separate from what happens in the public forum (the political). No doubt, too, there are some involved in the gay rights movement who bristle at the title, and various formulations of the idea—the truth—that we are more than sex have leapt to their lips. This book is, therefore, an answer to both audiences. To make the work as accessible as possible, I have used citation sparingly. The reader may rely upon the selected bibliography for those sources that have most informed my argument. Because this book is as much a political pamphlet as anything else, I have relied heavily on the historical and expository work of those authors listed there; I am in their debt.

The gay person in American society is as he is because his interpersonal sexual relationships have been politicized and used as an instrument of his domination by others. In the United States today, one's sexuality remains the chief factor in defining one's civic fitness and, indeed, one's entire humanity. If one falls into the disfavored sexual category—homosexual—one is automatically unfit to serve openly in one's country's armed forces. In most of the United States, one is not allowed to marry the person of one's choosing; one is unfit to adopt and raise children; one can be fired or not be hired in the first place. All of these things are very real possibilities simply if one is a gay person. To deny the politicization of sexuality in such circumstances is foolishness.

Social definition on the basis of sexual orientation is quintessentially political; in many ways, it is the heart of American politics today. Whether out of the closet or in, the gay person assumes a slotted role in a predefined power structure. The out person finds himself set against the predominating political grain, whereas the closeted gay person also fills a political role by accommodating the prevailing sociopolitical power structure. Even the most closeted of the closeted is not apolitical.

But there is another view of sexual politics—that of the gay rights movement as progressive social reengineering. Gays sexualize politics simply by bucking long-held notions of pathology and inferiority by claiming and asserting those rights held in common by other Americans. Thus, this book is also my attempt to articulate the current political position of the homosexual and to call for political attentiveness by those who have buried their heads, believing—like much of straight America—that what goes on behind the closed doors of the bedroom or, more aptly, the closed doors of America's closets doesn't affect their status as American citizens. My argument for collective concern and for the further emergence of a gay and lesbian ethos of public attentiveness is essentially political because it is bent toward the reshaping of public norms that ultimately define private life.

Today, America remains a place where virtually no act by a gay or lesbian person can be apolitical; simply because that act is performed by a gay or lesbian person, it takes on a dimension and meaning to the greater society that it otherwise would not have. The very act of publicly acknowledging oneself as gay or lesbian is itself a quintessentially political act, because it challenges the otherwise coerced definition of what it means to be a normal, natural person and a fully participating member of society. That very visibility provides the basis for the transformative politics discussed later, which is an overall cultural politic encompassing all those activities of the gay and lesbian person: art, literature, sports, business, education, spirituality, and otherwise conventional forms of politics.

A purely private reconciliation with one's homosexuality is an inadequate response to the political sexualization faced by the gay individual in the United States. Consequently, the first chapter of this book seeks to give definition and meaning to the otherwise amorphous concept of the closet and to address the need of closeted individuals to move outside the isolation and secrecy of the closet to claim their dignity and the rights concomitant with that dignity. Chapter 1 explores the historical foundations of the closet and the effects of the closet on the private and communal lives of gay people in America, and it makes a plea for honest and responsible living on a personal and civic level.

Chapter 2 discusses the religious factors that have resulted in the pariah status of gays and lesbians in the United States. The condemnation of same-sex sexuality as sinful and abominable is not historically static, nor is it based on some universal principle. Despite constitutional guarantees of a separation between religion and government, America is the only modern Western nation in which religion and politics remain extensively commingled. For that reason, chapter 2 explores the religious foundations of homophobia and the inescapable consequences of America's religiously infused politics, while offering a hopeful solution to the American religious dilemma.

Any understanding of the historical and contemporary position of an oppressed minority is virtually meaningless unless its ultimate end is to feed a healthy politics of social progression. Consequently, after outlining the position of the gay person in American society, chapter 3 frames a plea for political involvement and attentiveness to the public dimensions of homosexuality. And because a civil rights movement must, by its very nature, operate within the confines of the prevailing political system, some knowledge and understanding of the sociopolitical climate as it affects gays in the United States is imperative to the development of an effective politics. Thus, chapter 3 also outlines the institutional obstacles to successful gay politics and addresses the future prospects for equality.

Chapter 4 is a summation of the legitimate desires of gay people and an attempt to describe the necessary means of getting there.

Because this book is based, in large part, on my own experiences and observations, it is to some extent autobiographical. It may, therefore, seem to emphasize the experiences of gay men at the expense of a discussion of issues exclusively affecting lesbians in this country. To the extent that this is so, it was merely unavoidable. It certainly should not be taken as a suggestion that I do not feel that the plight of the lesbian is equally as important as the plight of the gay man in America.

It is my hope that this work will shed some light, for straight people, on gays as individuals rather than simply as political or legal lightning rods. It is also my hope that it will be enlightening for the gay reader, because the gay rights movement itself has been largely devoid of personal discourse. A necessary part of enlightenment is taking the unpleasant along with the pleasant. In this book, I discuss many unpleasant aspects of the gay experience. The knowledge void and, in some cases, willful ignorance have made the discussion of those things unavoidable. In discussing those things, however, my idea is not to project an utterly morbid outlook on gay life in America but rather to put forth some knowledge about the reality of being gay in America—and that reality in relation to gays and straights alike. I hope that, by discussing these unpleasant, unattractive aspects of our society, I will prove that the advancement of gay rights is good not only for gays but for everyone—for every member of our society.

Ultimately, of course, I realize the enormity of the problem of arguing for social change in an area in which feelings are as deeply entrenched as they are in the area of gay rights: One's opponents are not always willing to discuss and debate in good faith. In matters as politically, emotionally, and spiritually charged as gay rights, reason is often the missing ingredient. A huge contributing factor to the slow pace of gay advancement in this country is that, from the beginning, the debate has been dominated by people who have nothing at all to say. The content of their argument is a mystery to all but them, and they make no effort to say more than a bald assertion of their empty belief. But reason and truth are the enemies of the bigot. Thus, the goal of this work is to share some useful knowledge with the sympathetically inclined or impartial participant in the gay rights debate—they have been ignored for too long. It is with these individuals that the future of gay rights in this country rests. Filling the void with useful knowledge rather than empty rhetoric will arm these critical people with the information they need to spot the disingenuous argument of the bigot when confronted by it. Like Dr. Martin Luther King Jr., I believe that, when all is said and done, it is not "the violent actions and the vitriolic words of the bad people" that will be remembered but rather "the appalling silence and indifference of the good people." Surely, we will be asked to account not only for the misdeeds of the "children of darkness," but also for the "fears and apathy of the children of light."[1] Fears must be confronted. Only when the good people are given the necessary understanding can they be expected to break their silence.

CHAPTER 1

A World Not of Their Making

The Closet in American Life

*His remembrance shall perish from the earth and He shall have no name in the
street. He shall be driven from light into darkness, and chased out of the world.*

—Job 18:17–18

HISTORY, FOR ALL TOO MANY PEOPLE, is the convenient referent for a fact
or set of facts that has fallen into a void of unimportance, irrelevant
to modern concerns. The historical knowledge possessed by most Americans is sadly substandard, and gays as a community share this abysmal ap-
preciation of time gone by. But "[y]ou have to look at history as an
evolution of society," said Jean Chrétien, prime minister of Canada, after
his cabinet approved a policy to open marriage to gay couples.[1] Indeed, a
society pays a consuming price for failing to understand its own history. In
that spirit, understanding the closet as a cultural phenomenon necessitates
understanding the history that created the closet.

Unfortunately, there is much in American history to suggest that our
democratic social ideal is perhaps more the possession of theoreticians than
it is a practically attainable goal. By letter, the United States began as a society in which religious passion was kept separate from public reason and
separation of church and state was the benchmark. This much is enshrined
in that great monument of democracy, the Constitution.

The roots of what became American society, however, reach further than 1787 and the drafting of the Constitution; they reach back to groups like the Puritans, who came to America's shores in search of a place to practice a way of life so stern that even the Cromwellian harshness of their contemporary England was unacceptably lax. They migrated to Holland, but the Dutch of five centuries ago were too liberal to countenance the heavy-handed righteousness of the Puritans, whom they promptly expelled.

Like most religious fundamentalists, the Puritans were inclined to see God as an evasive being who created a labyrinth of rules to thwart the petty human's attempt to attain everlasting life. For them, the charity of Jesus was a footnote, whereas the sum of biblical wisdom was to be found in the severer passages of the Old Testament and in the unforgiving dicta of Saint Paul. Accordingly, because adultery was forbidden by commandment and because Saint Paul specifically denounced homosexuality, the Puritans promptly criminalized such abominations in the theocracy they were eventually free to create in the American wilderness.

The Puritans' rigorous persecution of the sinner—in an effort to save his soul by force, if he would not do so volitionally—developed into a legal moralism that American society has never quite been able to rise above. The result: American penal history, and even modern criminal law, are the scandal of the free world. Only in the twenty-first century were gay Americans afforded the basic rights of sexual privacy and bodily autonomy by order of the U.S. Supreme Court.[2] Yet since its earliest days, the republic has been a place of sharp division between the scarlet letter of the law and the actual practice of citizens' private lives. The states' police powers over morality resulted in a host of laws governing sex, which, while often textually neutral (that is, applying to both heterosexual and homosexual conduct), were usually applied inequitably to punish the vilest offender, the sexual deviant—the homosexual.

Because of this concerted effort to stamp out homosexuality for the good of the greater society, homosexual history in the United States must be pulled from a past of degradation and shame. We might say that our history itself has been buried in the back of our communal closet. Despite this, once uncovered, the history is a vital one from which much can be learned about the present-day place of the gay individual in American society. Since the 1970s, a burgeoning body of literature has emerged, and many schools and universities now devote courses and seminars specifically to gay studies. Numerous historians and commentators have documented gay history. The record of the closet, pulled from centuries of secrecy and isolation, brings to light a fascinating social history of survival and, finally, self-actualization.

WHERE WE COME FROM . . .

As long as there have been people in North America, there have been homosexuals. Although much of the cultural memory has been blotted out by homophobic whites and Christianized Native Americans, the explorers and missionaries who first came to the New World encountered Native American androgynes wholly accepted and playing vital roles in tribal life. The French term *berdache* was used to describe Native American men who dressed as women and performed the roles of women in public and private life. In many tribes, some women fought in battles and were feared and revered as effective warriors, whereas some men expressed effeminate mannerisms and contributed to the artistic and cultural life of the tribe. Ruth Benedict, an anthropologist, noted the comfortable niches created for gender-role variants who would today be known as homosexual.[3] The Native American cultural view of the gay person focused on gender-role identity and not exclusively on sexual habits.

The coming of the white colonialist to America brought not only the oppression of the Native American but also a differing view of sexuality and gender identity. America became the escape of the Pilgrims and other puritanical groups whose rigid religious legalism propelled them outside of a changing European society. Left to their own devices, these groups created a host of ostensibly Bible-based regulations governing sex and morality. Puritanical society emphasized submission of women to their husbands and the sinfulness of nonprocreative sexual activity. Many sex acts that did not come to procreative ends were made capital offenses.

But if America's early fundamentalists used the Bible to craft oppressive laws, they did so with as much of a spirit of equality as oppression can be said to command. When they outlawed sodomy, they forbade it equally between the sexes. Their concern was the sinfulness of all nonprocreative sexual activity; therefore, the homosexual was not relegated to an especially reprehensible class of offender by the letter of the law. For the most part, homosexuals of this early period did not identify themselves as intrinsically different from heterosociety, nor did they have opportunities to identify with others like themselves. They most often married and had children, indulging their homosexual inclinations at great risk.

The Industrial Revolution that swept the United States at the end of the nineteenth century, however, changed the ways in which homosexuals lived and related to one another. People left the isolation of country and village and came to the city, where life was freer and association easier. The large population and the confined geography of the city increased the chances of discovering others with similar sexual identities and inclinations. This confluence of circumstances inevitably led to the birth of the gay subculture, which survives in a very real way today.

If the city provided gay individuals with the opportunity to connect with others like themselves, life outside the infant homosexual community was still harsh. Information about homosexuality was scarce; most individuals continued to think of their sexuality not in terms of natural orientation but of sinfulness and deviance. Homosexuality was a legally punishable offense, and it would remain so until the twenty-first century. Self-censorship of the press contributed to a lack of understanding. When gay-related news was reported, it was usually bad, and even then details were glossed over and euphemisms employed. Even the trial of Oscar Wilde for sodomy in Britain, which so sensationalized Europe, was given short shrift in the U.S. media.

As the twentieth century dawned, the medical community became the greatest enemy of the homosexual. As psychiatry grew to become a respectable field of medicine, psychiatric theories about gay deviance and its curability circulated throughout the country. Young men and, to a lesser degree, women were subjected to untold horrors in the search for a cure—including chemically induced convulsions, electroshock therapy, castration for men, sterilization, lobotomy, and other surgical nightmares.[4]

Within the subculture, however, gays could find some measure of normalcy and escape from repression. In a study of pre–World War II gay males in New York City, George Chauncey described a thriving gay community situated primarily in ethnic and working-class neighborhoods. Gays existing within that community developed a self-contained society with its own language, social norms, and group associations. Sexual inverts like Ralph Werther, who wrote an autobiography describing his life in the gay subculture of New York City in the 1890s, were allowed to live relatively open lives. When forced to interact with heterosociety, the gays of the subculture devised ways of distinguishing themselves and identifying with one another. Red ties and bleached hair, for example, signified membership in the gay community.

LEGAL OPPRESSION . . .

The penal code of New York in the 1880s was typical of post–Civil War lawmaking. It placed a heavy emphasis on public morals, prohibiting rape, abduction, carnal abuse of children, abortion, bigamy, incest, sodomy, indecent exposure, possession or publication of obscene materials, and keeping a disorderly house as "crimes against the person and against public decency and good morals."[5] But to the extent that same-sex sexual activity was penalized under this regime, it was penalized indirectly. Even the sodomy laws, enacted by all but three states in the Union, were rarely applied to same-sex individuals. This is not to say that same-sex activity was unknown or sanctioned; Walt Whitman had already published the homoerotic poems of *Leaves of Grass,* which were met with a great deal of scandal. But there was no attempt at legal suppression. If the society of the middle and late 1800s did not sanction same-sex eroticism, neither did that society overtly penalize it.

In the decades after the Civil War, the country began a campaign for homogeneity that threatened the gay subculture and eventually drove it completely underground—into the emerging closet. Soon, civic groups began to form in order to quell sexual deviance, a job they believed the law was not doing satisfactorily. New York City's Comstock Society (the Society for the Suppression of Vice) was founded in 1872 for such a purpose. By the 1890s, the Comstock Society was assisting police in monitoring degenerate behavior in the subculture's principal areas. The Society, its outrage seething, urged officials to use the sodomy law to combat sexual deviants. Anthony Comstock, from whom the Society took its name, had this to say after reading Ralph Werther's autobiographical account: "These inverts are not fit to live with the rest of mankind. They ought to have branded in their foreheads the word 'Unclean,' and as the lepers of old, they ought to cry 'Unclean! Unclean!' as they go about, and instead of the [sodomy] law making twenty years imprisonment the penalty for their crime, it ought to be imprisonment for life."[6] Driven by intensifying social outrage and a millennialist revival of puritanical morality, the law began to change toward a more pointed and effective suppression of sexual deviance.

Antisodomy statutes were the most effective mechanism by which government sought to restrain homosexual conduct. However, most sodomy laws covered only anal sex, and prosecutions were mainly of opposite-sex offenders.[7] But by the late nineteenth and early twentieth centuries, many states changed their sodomy laws to make it easier to target gays; legislatures simply rewrote their sodomy or buggery statutes to encompass oral sex.[8] In other states, the definition was expanded by judicial decision.[9] In others still, a more indirect approach was taken; Massachusetts, for instance, made it a crime to be a "lewd, wanton, or lascivious person."[10]

Once sodomy laws encompassed oral sex, they were more easily applied to prostitutes, especially male prostitutes who dressed as women and offered oral pleasure to their customers. It also made lesbians vulnerable to prosecutions for sodomy, a virtual impossibility before, although lesbians still accounted for a mere fraction of the sodomy arrests of the period.[11] Sodomy laws, however, still proved unwieldy; because they carried felony penalties, their use was proscribed by procedural safeguards like indictment and trial by jury. Aggressive laws against cross-dressing were implemented to take up the slack. Homosexuals joined the ranks of Joan of Arc and Elizabeth Cady Stanton as degenerates for wearing *dress not belonging to his or her sex*. A proliferation of disorderly conduct laws further added to the arsenal of gay suppression.

Furthermore, the psychological quackery of the early twentieth century fueled many Americans' suspicions that homosexuals were sexual predators out to defile their children. The linkage of homosexuality to pedophilia reached hysteria by the 1930s. Obscenity laws were increasingly employed to suppress literature branded degenerate, like British novelist Radclyffe Hall's lesbian-themed work, *The Well of Loneliness*.

INTO THE CLOSET . . .

An aggressive social campaign against homosexuals influenced the development of the law; the law, consequently, perpetuated misunderstanding and restricted opportunities for change of societal attitudes. As the law became increasingly oppressive, the gay subculture enjoyed by the likes of Ralph Werther was driven completely underground.

World War II was a watershed in the evolution of gay culture. Thousands of men entered gender-segregated environments for the first time. Although there was screening to avoid enlisting homosexuals in the military, most gays did not dare reveal their sexual orientation and joined the swelling ranks sent to the European and Pacific theaters, perhaps disproportionately, given the military's preference for single, childless men. Living and fighting closely together, these men had a great opportunity to form intimate friendships, and the close proximity permitted sexual activity for which there would otherwise have been limited opportunity. The cost of getting caught was, of course, dire. Suspected gays were dishonorably discharged and subjected to courts-martial and fearsome psychiatric examinations. Women, too, in their new roles in industry had opportunity to pursue their sexual desires without fear of family or marital pressure. The Women's Army Corps, with one hundred fifty thousand members, attracted a large percentage of lesbians.

As the homophobic furor escalated, no one was safe from its repercussions. When in 1941 FBI Director J. Edgar Hoover gained information pertaining to Undersecretary of State Sumner Welles, he warned President Franklin Roosevelt of the national security risk Welles posed, considering his susceptibility to blackmail. Hoover and his chief counsel, Roy Cohn, made homosexuality an issue of national security and ensured decades of oppressive policy based upon that lie. When the draft was reinstated, men, and eventually women, were explicitly asked about their sexual proclivity. As the war wore on and the need of manpower became more desperate, the strategy of the military was to medicalize homosexuality rather than to criminalize it. If offenders were not encumbered by some more manifest crime, like rape, they were given therapy for their condition but were not immediately discharged from the service. Court-martial and discharge, however, remained the official policy of the military.

But the tolerance born of necessity during the war quickly evaporated at the war's close. Instead of rewards for valiant service, the end of World War II brought an unprecedented purge of gays from the military, which was but a precursor to the severer crackdowns of the 1950s. Thousands of gay men and women were discharged. Rather than returning to their homes in disgrace, many servicemen and women relocated to urban areas and became part of the gay subculture.

When heterosociety recovered from the shock of war, reactionaries wasted no time in returning society to the prewar status quo. They did this at any expense. Heterosexual men, returning from war to find their hegemony threatened, harangued liberated women and homosexuals as subversive and included them in the greater anticommunist campaign. They were made part and parcel of the heartless, godless communism that fifties reactionaries saw themselves pitted against. The paranoid McCarthyism of the day asserted that gays were security risks, easily susceptible to blackmail because of their subversive lifestyles. This era was the cradle of the security risk argument used as justification for the military's gay ban. Like today, the government inexplicably discharged openly gay men and women, despite the apparent blackmail threat having been removed by their coming out. Hoover and Cohn were employed to ferret out the sex perverts holding government jobs. In 1951, Hoover had identified 406 such perverts in government employ. In a sad twist of irony, both Hoover and Cohn were gay. Senator Joseph McCarthy, himself, is rumored to have been gay. As Arthur Lipkin has written, "the level of internalized hatred and hypocrisy in these witch-hunts is stupefying."[12] In 1953, President Eisenhower issued Executive Order 10450, formally dismissing gays from government service.

Amid this gloom, the fifties saw the first large-scale and concerted movement toward legal reform. On April 25, 1955, a committee of the American Law Institute (ALI), a think tank of legal practitioners, judges, and academicians, presented the Model Penal Code to the whole of the ALI. The purpose of the code was to serve as a model for state legislatures for reform of their laws. The drafters proposed the decriminalization of sodomy between consenting adults, stating that "the Code does not attempt to use the power of the state to enforce purely moral or religious standards. . . . Such matters are best left to religious, educational and other influences." There was, of course, contention over such a marked departure from the Calvinist sentiment then reigning in American jurisprudence. ALI member John Parker answered the drafters thus: "There are many things that are denounced by the criminal code in order that society may know that the state disapproves. When we fly in the face of public opinion, as evidenced by the code of every state in this union, we are not proposing a code which will commend itself to the thoughtful." The estimable Learned Hand, however, had the final say: "Criminal law which is not enforced practically is much worse than if it was not on the books at all. I think homosexuality is a matter of morals, a matter very largely of taste, and it is not a matter that people should be put in prison about." Hand's position was adopted by the institute.[13]

But the Model Penal Code was just that—a model—and its immediate effect on sexual oppression was minimal. Persecution of gays continued. The FBI compiled lists of suspected sexual deviants. Police regularly raided gay and lesbian bars. Even parties at private residences were broken up and arrests were made. In the same year the Model Penal Code was presented, after the arrest of three men for having sex with teenage boys, fourteen hundred residents of Boise, Idaho, were called to testify as to their sexual orientation and that of their neighbors. Countless men fled the city, not because they were child molesters, but for fear of being exposed as homosexuals.

Newspapers frequently printed the names of alleged homosexuals apprehended in police raids. Gays everywhere were subject to victimization and violence by thugs and police alike. Also in 1955, Harry Hay, founder of the now legendary Mattachine Society, one of the earliest organizations for the promotion of gay rights, was called to testify before the House Committee on Un-American Activities. The message ringing in Hay's summons was clear: Homosexuality is Un-American.

WHERE WE ARE:
THE CONSTRUCT OF THE CLOSET . . .

The events and the collective consciousness formed in the American 1950s framed the closet, and they are still the events most illustrative of the closet and its operation in this country today. One cannot watch Tony Kushner's *Angels in America* and fail to be impressed by its portrayal of the complex system of the closet in American society. Certainly, the story of the Mormon character realizing his sexuality is compelling, but the character that stands out most in my mind is that of the aforementioned Roy Cohn, chief henchman of former FBI Director J. Edgar Hoover. Cohn's story is tragic. In order to rise to the top, he had to play the game instituted by heterosociety; that is, he had to be heterosexual—at least in every outward appearance. So Cohn resorted to the closet in order to publicly suppress his homosexual identity. For many in the closet, cheap and anonymous sex is a modus operandi; and this was true of Cohn, whose death from AIDS is poignantly portrayed in *Angels in America*.

Cohn's story is just one in a web of closeted tragedy. Cohn colluded with Hoover, himself homosexual, but who, nevertheless, tenaciously exposed and rooted out homosexuals from the civil service. Much of that activity was prompted by the hysteria spawned by Senator Joseph McCarthy, who was also probably gay. When Washington's backroom rumors were made public by journalist Hank Greenspun, McCarthy considered suing for libel but was dissuaded when he realized that doing so would force him to answer questions about his sexuality. Instead, in an effort to curtail the damage, he married his secretary and adopted a child.

These men are very visible examples of individuals living life in the closet and of the hypocrisy that goes along with that life. But they are certainly not exceptional; every gay youth is introduced early on to the closet. I was introduced at an early age. My earliest memories of social instruction are my mother's telling me that I acted like a sissy and that I should try not to walk so funny or hang around with girls so much. She was horrified to find that I preferred dressing Barbie to racing Hot Wheels cars. She didn't want me to go to my grandmother's house because she let me play with dolls. I was forced into a host of machismo-infused activities. First, there was tee-ball and baseball; I prayed for rain every Saturday. When I was a dismal failure at baseball, basketball was forced on me—anything to maintain the façade.

It didn't work.

Children are extraordinarily perceptive individuals; they often know who the gay children are even before the parents of gay children know. They can also be extraordinarily cruel. The name-calling, for me, started almost immediately: sissy, queer, fag. I bonded mostly with girls because, I think, of the common oppression factor. And girls, in general, are a lot more forgiving of the unorthodox than are little boys.

Moreover, my church was telling me that my very nature was sinful. Of course they couched this a bit: they told me that acting on the impulses was wrong, if perhaps my just being gay wasn't. But even at age eleven or twelve, I knew quite well that what they meant was that being gay was a sin, no matter how they decorated the proposition. Even being effeminate was sinful. In fact, in the King James Bible, the only version of the Bible to which I was ever exposed (I once attended a tent revival meeting where the presiding minister passed a wastebasket and announced that anyone who was carrying a version of "the Word" besides the King James version should promptly deposit their filth in the trash where it belonged—prompting me to wonder why England's gay monarch is the final word on the holy Word), the very word that has been translated "homosexual" in more modern translations (I Corinthians 6:9) is translated "effeminate." So even if I wasn't gay, as my mother said, I acted gay, and that was enough to give me a good whiff of burning sulfur when I laid my head on the pillow at night. Instead of trying to escape from the tortures of religion, however, I ran full force into them, for I was an exceptionally religious child. I decided that if I were just good enough, just faithful enough, God would remove the scourge from me. But I did not have the constancy of Job: Nightly I prayed, "Why did you do this to me?" and "Please take it all away."

Finally, I decided that, if I had to be gay, the real sin was committing gay acts and that I would just bear my cross and persevere through a life of celibacy. I might be gay, but I damned well didn't have to admit it. Even later, during my college years, when I was safely ensconced within a group of friends who would not have cared about my sexual orientation, I routinely answered in the negative their questions about my preferences. The mind-set of the closet had been so firmly engrained in me that, even when circumstances permitted, I could not be open about my sexuality; it was just too hard, too difficult. One of my chief regrets is that I lost my closest friend when she discovered in later years, from a third party, that I had been dishonest with her about that core part of my life. But the closet was comfortable, familiar, and safe. I do not dispute that one is much happier freed from its constraints, like the bird flown from the cage, but stepping out into the world uncensored is no small feat of courage.

Whatever my mother's reasons were for so warping my conception of sexual orientation, she must have known these cruel realities of the world. She must have known the hard road the homosexual faces in school, in relationships, in employment, in family. I myself often have thought about how I would feel were one of my children to come to me and say that he or she was gay. Naturally, I wouldn't be hampered by all the social stigma and religious bigotry that colored my mother's view of things, but I wouldn't be elated. I know the difficult road.

And that road does not necessarily brighten just because one manages to break out of the closet. During law school, I did what was expected of me; I applied for legal internships and jobs. By this point, I was making these applications as an out gay man, and that significantly altered the rules. At one interview, an older male partner commented on my resume. He noted my affiliation with the American Civil Liberties Union and a gay youth group and then quipped: "What are you people complaining about now . . . whether two lesbians can be married in Wait Chapel?" (referring to a much-contested ceremony that took place at the chapel of the university where I studied). "Actually," I shot back, "we hashed that out a few years ago—and we won." The interview went downhill from there. I could recount various other, more subtle examples.

A friend of mine went to work for a large law firm in Atlanta and then quit because of harassment over his orientation. Employers may follow the trend of extending benefits to the life partners of gays and lesbians, but they do not care to have the recipients of those benefits show up at the office

Christmas party. For many gays, it is easier to secret their private lives away than to be scrutinized in the office fishbowl. The closet is a comfortable place (even if that comfort is illusory) for the gay individual, but it is the comfort zone of heterosociety, as well. Many heterosexuals prefer the homosexual in the closet. Although much of liberal heterosociety must be commended for the advances made in gay rights over the past decades (for these advances could not have taken place without our straight brothers and sisters), the "tolerance" versus "acceptance" model that emerged in liberal politics is a chief, if largely unconscious, factor contributing to the perpetuation of the closet. Although progressive straights are willing to tolerate gay people, they are not always as ready to see them garner the same rights as heterosociety—they are not ready for wholesale acceptance.

When *Lawrence v. Texas*, the Supreme Court case that invalidated the nation's remaining sodomy laws, came down, I read as much newspaper coverage on the subject as I could get my hands on. For me, the most intriguing aspect of that coverage was the inevitable poll: Was *Lawrence v. Texas* a good decision or a bad decision? I was surprised to see the overwhelming response that *Lawrence* was a good decision. Even the *Winston-Salem Journal*, my local paper, in an area that is not a bastion of liberalism, reported that *Lawrence* was a good decision. But the good was a qualified good. Those polled often replied, "I don't care what gays do in the privacy of their bedrooms, and the government has no business there; but I hope this doesn't lead to gay marriage." The message was clear. Gays should have their "privacy," but gays should keep their sexuality "private," hidden from view in the closet. Privacy was the key word. Those who follow legal developments, especially developments in constitutional law, recognize that the Supreme Court often is not ahead of the constitutional curve but often is a lagging indicator of what majority America has decided the content of a particular constitutional norm should be. Indeed, *Lawrence* is a reflection of the accuracy of that theory. The *Lawrence* Court carefully indicated that it was not talking about gay marriage, and the American public was lockstep behind (or in front) of it.

But, of course, the marriage revolution did follow. Gays began to assert their equal rights with regard to marriage. In the wake of *Lawrence*, a measurable backward slide in majoritarian opinion was detectable. Polls (for what polls are worth) show that a majority of Americans do not favor gay marriage; they might even support a constitutional amendment to preclude it (though, as I will explore later, I doubt that they really understand what such an amendment means).

Some of this, I think, is attributable to the human desire to "root for the underdog." When progress is made, it is less entertaining to champion the downtrodden. A more likely explanation is that straight people don't understand the closet. As Michelangelo Signorile has said, "Because heterosexuality is the order of things, many heterosexuals think that they never discuss their sexuality. They say gays who come out [and demand their rights] are going too far, making an issue of their sexuality when heterosexuals don't." Signorile observed in his book *Queer in America* that "[t]hose heterosexuals don't realize that they routinely discuss aspects of their own sexuality every day: telling coworkers about a vacation they took with a lover; explaining to their bosses that they're going through a rough divorce; bragging to friends about a new romance."[14] When gays attempt to do the same, there is discomfort among heterosexuals. Coming out of the closet is okay. It might even be a good thing. But coming too far out of the closet is just too much.

Exactly what one is coming out of is not easily explicated. In terms of a referent, the closet is difficult to define. Practically every gay and straight person would have a different answer to the question "What is the closet?" Likewise, the question "What does it mean to 'come out' of the closet?" would elicit a myriad of responses. Being out does not mean shouting one's sexual orientation from the rooftops. Even at the most individualistic level, there are remarkably few people of even the most open sexual orientation who are not deliberately in the closet with someone personally, economically, or institutionally important to them. The closet remains a shaping presence, no matter how fortunate the support of the immediate community. Signorile has written that "[b]eing out of the closet means not thinking about it at all."[15] I cannot agree with this proposition because I believe it is imperative that we "think about it" so that we are not lulled into complacency in our fight for equality.

Consequently, I would say that being out constitutes a discernible shift in thought patterns. It means a gradual breaking down of the structures of deceit that one has employed in order to live life. It means not worrying that friends and colleagues will discover your sexuality; it means not hiding papers and letters; it means showing up with one's partner at company functions; it means refusing to be lonely, secretive, and unfulfilled. Coming out is the crossing and re-crossing of so many lines drawn in the sand—sometimes it simply means not hiding.

The closet is the anathema of honest living. The dishonesty it fosters destroys the character of all those who come in contact with it. As gay novelist Christopher Isherwood has written, "While you're being persecuted, you hate what's happening to you, you hate the people who are making it happen; you're in a world of hate." In his book *God Has A Dream*, Bishop Desmond Tutu makes a similar observation about the apartheid regime in South Africa that I think also adequately describes the effects of the closet in the lives of gay people. Tutu writes: "In South Africa, the victims of the apartheid system often ended up internalizing the definition the system had of them. They began to wonder whether they might not perhaps be somehow as their masters and mistresses defined them. Thus they would frequently accept that the values of the domineering class were worth striving after. And then the awful demons of self-hate and self-contempt, a hugely negative self-image, took their place in the center of the victim's being. These demons are corrosive of proper self-love and self-assurance, and eat away at the very vitals of the victim's being." In the same way, the complicity of gays in the secrets and lies of the closet makes us agents in the denial of our own dignity.[16]

For example, a couple of years ago I became acquainted with a brilliant young gay man. Professional, successful, intellectual, he moved to North Carolina from Dallas, Texas, where he had left an eight-year relationship with a man of equal professional stature and intellectual caliber. Rarely did we meet when he did not bemoan his life in North Carolina. More than once he specifically employed the word "miserable" as a descriptor for what he referred to as a "lonely existence." He explained to me how much in love he was with the man he had left in Dallas and that his Dallas love was pressuring him to return to Texas and move in with him. For career reasons, he explained, neither of them would leave his residence and permanently go to the other.

At first I was irritated with him. He had—just waiting for him it seemed—what most of us desperately desire: someone who loves us and wants us with them. I felt he was simply letting his life be dictated by lust for the almighty dollar at the expense of true love. But, as is often the case with first-blush impressions, my assessment of the situation was not entirely accurate. As he began to share more particulars about his relationship, I realized just how unhealthy that relationship was. I learned that, for six years, while my friend lived in North Carolina, he traveled twice monthly from Charlotte to Dallas to see his partner. Yet the partner never acknowledged the relationship to his family. My friend was always simply a buddy, a friend from college. In addition, his partner requested that my friend not be honest about his sexuality to his own family and friends, for fear that accusations of homosexuality would then be made against the partner.

On his many visits to Texas, my friend often was included in the partner's family events, but always only as the ubiquitous buddy. During many family events, my friend had to endure hostile comments like "AIDS is God's punishment for the faggot" from his partner's homophobic father, all the while sitting silently, denying his own sexuality. At the worst moments, the son joined in his father's vitriolic words. In spite of this, my friend was very much in love with the man from Dallas; so much so that the very thought of him dashed all hope for another relationship.

I realized that this relationship had a death grip on my friend's soul. I thought that if he went out, met more gay friends, and saw healthy relationships, he would be able to leave his Dallas partner behind and move on with his life. But so insular was their professional community that my friend lived a completely closeted life even in Charlotte, for fear that openness would cause reverberations in Dallas. As time wore on, he became more sullen; he talked more frequently of returning to Dallas. I tried to persuade him that if he was unhappy with his relationship from a distance, his problems would only be magnified when they were brought into closer proximity. I asked him to think about what it would mean for him to move to Dallas as the platonic roommate rather than as the romantic lover. But my words were to no avail. My friend repeatedly told me how well his partner treated him when they were alone together, how sweet and gentle and kind he was. Eventually, we lost touch, and I heard that his career carried him elsewhere. I have no doubt that, if his relationship remains intact, he is as miserable there as he was here.

My friend failed to realize that the qualitative measure of how someone treats us is to be found not only in the way we are treated behind the closed doors of the closet but also in the way we are treated, appreciated, and praised in public places. The inability of many gays to recognize this fundamental life tenet is testament to the insidiousness of the closet. Too many gay relationships are relationships of secrecy and distrust. Romances that should be vivid and robust instead flounder and are left etiolated because the closet does not afford them the light and air they need to thrive. In its

campaign against gay marriage, society focuses on the vacuity of gay relationships, branding them inconsequential and incapable of making any positive contribution to the heterosexual world. We perpetuate these heinous
fallacies by treating our most intimate relationships as irrelevant to our own
lives, by secreting them in the closet.

It has been said that the opposite of love is not hate; it is selfishness. The
true lover elevates the feelings of his beloved above all else, certainly above
the bigotries and petty prejudices of the world. But the closet stifles honest
expression, and self-censorship and secrecy take its place. A love kept secret is not a love made sweeter; it is a fraud. In such relationships, one is left
to wonder and to doubt one's status. Rather than a source of stability and
strength, the secret romance is one of uneasiness, disillusionment, and doubt.
If the worth of our love is cast in doubt, eventually our own self-worth is
put in doubt; there is no greater weapon than self-loathing, no greater in-
surance of failure than self-doubt. Such is the power of the closet. The
closet does not create mere passive victims, stripped of their dignity by
forces outside their control. Instead, the closet makes us each complicit in
its dignity-robbing operations. Ultimately, *we* make the choice to be other
than we are, to remain less than whole; and through our deliberative complicity in the circle of dishonesty maintaining heterosexual dominance, the
choice is, thereby, all the more wounding, the more devastating.

THE DOOR AJAR . . .

But with little more effort than throwing open the door (this is not to
say that refusing to hide requires no effort—on the contrary it sometimes
requires extraordinary effort) great things can be achieved. I, for example,
entered law school determined to be myself. Attending law school in the
southern United States, I had reservations about conservatism and bigotry
but I hid nothing. If not in all aspects of my life, at school I was completely
open. To my happy surprise, I was received well. I became the unique person everyone wanted to know. If only on a shallow level by some, I was wel-
comed by everyone.

Everyone, that is, except one man in the third-year class. This particular
man would have none of me. He was dark and muscular and beautiful, and
I sensed that he felt that any pleasantry shared between us would be interpreted as an unwelcome advance by one or both of us. For that reason, I sur-
mised, he remained cold. There was even a flicker of hostility behind his

dark eyes, though it never came to the surface. When I smiled or spoke to him he never returned my cordiality. When I tried to start a conversation, he seemed annoyed at my intrusion into his solitude. In fairness, he was not particularly warm toward anyone, but his distaste for me was pronounced. Eventually, I gave up trying to win him over and kept my distance.

A year passed, and his class was graduating. As was our habit, all the students were gathered in a local bar one night shortly before graduation. I was propped against a pool table when I suddenly noticed him, determination in his eyes, coming at me through clouds of tobacco smoke. Immediately I steeled myself, for I had no idea what was coming. Instead of insult, he gently put his hand on my shoulder and said, "I just wanted you to know that before I met you, I couldn't conceive of having a gay friend. But having known you, I see what I've been missing by automatically dismissing everyone who is different from me. The school needs more people like you."

I was so stupefied that I could barely manage a weak "thank you." Quite unconsciously, I had succeeded in opening this man's mind to different possibilities—to the shared humanity in gay and straight alike. I had abandoned my campaign to win him over long before, but by simply being myself I had, in fact, won him over. Recalling that episode, I realize that we make a difference, often unawares, simply by being *willing* to make a difference.

Later, I shared that insight with a group of undergraduate students at the university where I work. I was invited to speak, as part of a panel, to the campus Gay-Straight Student Alliance. There was a surprisingly healthy turnout, which naturally pleased me. The topic was being gay in the workplace.

My pleasure at the turnout quickly turned to chagrin as I heard the first panelist speak. A business professor (himself gay) proceeded to tell these young, soon-to-be college graduates, that it was perfectly acceptable to hide their orientation, in effect, to live double lives. Heads nodded as the students seemed to indicate their agreement with the acceptability of the closet. When my turn came, I was indignant. I was outraged that anyone would tell these young people, the future of gay rights, that they could— that, in fact, it would be preferable if they did—hide in the closet. But I realized that a diatribe would compromise my voice with the students, so I began by calmly explaining that not everyone was fortunate enough to end up in a career situation as comfortable as mine. Academe, especially the right institution, is the freest and most open of environments. I also told them that all people have areas of their lives in which they are understandably less comfortable—or not comfortable at all. But then I patiently informed them of what I perceive to be the duty of every gay person: Unless a particular situation absolutely prohibits it, gay people have the *obligation* to share their lives with their coworkers. We should share with those with whom we probably spend as much time as with anybody the joys and the problems that come along with being gay. We should share this, I continued, not militantly but in the natural, inevitable way that colleagues share their lives. Usually, we come to see, as do they, that our lives really aren't that different. The recognition of our common humanity not only improves our relationships with our colleagues but also does much to advance gay rights. Through openness, we promote not tolerance, but understanding.

And understanding is key.

It is much more difficult to vote to deprive certain people of basic rights—the right to marry or to have a family or to be free from discrimination in employment—when you recognize that those measures directly affect someone you know, even like. Simply stated, it is much harder to hate someone you like or, at least, respect.

I then shared the story of my law school colleague's conversion. Afterward, a young woman approached me and said, "You know, you're right. If we hide and cower in the closet, nothing will ever change." She was most definitely right. Change often does not come in a deluge, but in a ceaseless trickle. The change to gay acceptance will come gradually, as more people are exposed to gays as emotional and moral equals; thereby, they will be unable to divorce themselves from our common humanity. As acknowledgement of this humanity becomes part of their lives, those who otherwise have been obtuse to the casual accidents of gay life will be unable to maintain their indifference. As author Wendell Berry has written concerning his return to his native Kentucky after an urban sojourn, "When I lived in other places I looked on their evils with the curious eye of a traveler; I was not responsible for them; it cost me nothing to be a critic, for I had not been there long, and I did not feel that I would stay. But here, now that I am both native and citizen, there is no immunity to what is wrong."[17] The same is true of the straight person who interacts with the gay person, not as a passing curiosity, but as a participating member in the experiences of every day. Our openness to those around us will prohibit them from denying their own complicity in the human wrongs committed in the quietness of their implicit approbation of silence. Through our openness to those around us, the indurate observer becomes the invested participant. Everyday activism, even if it is simply being open to those around us, is the key to a better future.

THE MIND-SET OF THE CLOSET . . .

Many in heterosociety simply cannot understand the closet because they have never been subject to its constraints. Because heterosociety is the majority, dominant society, many straights genuinely believe that they never make an issue of their sexuality and they cannot understand why gay people want to make an issue of theirs. To the chagrin of much of heterosociety, the love that once dared not speak its name has become increasingly vocal. "You are exaggerating," I hear from many straight people when I explain to them that, in virtually every aspect of life in this country, gay people are told what they can do and when they can do it—in short, who they can be.

Many straights don't realize that they are making an issue of their sexuality when they walk down a public sidewalk holding hands, when they discuss their family vacation around the office water cooler, when they send out Christmas cards with their spouse, or when they engage in any number of other activities that, at least implicitly, reveal their sexuality. The fact that these things are such a part of the normal order of life that they are given no thought underscores the sharp contrast between those living life as heterosexuals and those living it as homosexuals. Even the small, everyday actions that compose life suddenly acquire earth-moving significance when they come from gay actors. Heterosexuals feel they are having, as one e-mail I received from an angry woman put it, homosexuality "shoved in [their] faces."

Many heterosexuals are so used to second-class citizenship for gays that they view any demand for mere equality as a demand for special rights. Coming out is, therefore, a threat to their own rights and power structures. This is made plain in the debate over gays in the military.

In August 2002, the U.S. military was allowed to recruit at Harvard Law School's Office of Career Services for the first time since the school had instituted a ban on military recruitment through the career services office more than twenty years before to protest the military's antigay hiring policies. Previously, the school had complied with the Solomon Amendment, by which federal funds can be denied to schools that openly disrupt military recruitment, by allowing the military to recruit through a student organization. But with the advent of the George W. Bush administration and heightened military recruitment activities in the wake of 9/11, the U.S. Air Force threatened to institute proceedings against the law school that could have resulted in the loss of $328 million in federal funding to the university if the Department of Defense found them in violation. A network of twenty-five law schools and nine hundred law professors moved to block application of the amendment in federal court. A 2–1 ruling by the U.S. Court of Appeals for the Third Circuit, on November 29, 2004, blocked enforcement of the amendment in the Third Circuit. In March 2006, the decision of the appeals court was reversed by a unanimous Supreme Court.

As incensing as the military's ban can be for gays and lesbians, it is important to step back and understand what is really going on. During President Clinton's tenure, former senator and Arizona Republican Barry Goldwater commented in the *Washington Post* that "[l]ifting the ban on gays in the military isn't exactly nothing, but it's pretty damned close . . . If I were in the Senate today, I would rise on the Senate floor in support of our commander in chief. He may be a Democrat, but he happens to be right on this question."[18] Goldwater was referring to President Clinton's effort to lift the ban. Clinton, however, admittedly under a firestorm of protest from Congress, disappointed gays and lesbians by backing off his promise to lift the ban; instead, he instituted the compromise "don't ask, don't tell" policy.

Why was the ban instituted in the first place? And why wasn't it lifted as promised?

The hubbub about gays in the ranks is about more than preserving the decorum of the communal shower. Several years ago I received a beautiful birthday gift from a group of friends, a Tiffany vase in a flower motif—pansies. I thought this was an appropriate gift because *pansy* is a derivative of the French verb *penser*, which means "to think," and every time I look at the vase I think of the thoughtful people who gave it to me. I also got a chuckle out of the gift because everyone knows that the gay man is sometimes called "pansy" in order to indicate that he is puny and weak. I'm not sure where this interesting bit of linguistics comes from, because the horticulturist knows that the real pansy, a lovely flower, is a hardy little devil that can be buried in the snows of upcountry North Carolina only to raise its proud head again after the thaw. Few plants, and certainly fewer people, can boast that sort of tenacity.

By this point the gentle reader is no doubt asking, "What in hell does this have to do with gays in the military?!" The answer is this: It seems to me that within the military there is fear of a shift in the traditional dominance of machismo, which heretofore has reigned supreme in the armed forces as in most of society. The gay man, conventional wisdom goes, is puny, weak, and girlish—a pansy—not fit for armed service. The straight man, by contrast, is strong and robust, an engineered warrior. The bigot thrives on difference, real or perceived, and his hatred is particularly dependent upon it in order to survive. He is especially pleased when he can point to a long history of bigotry to validate his continuing position as a bigot.

This fear was sorely evident when the U.S. Supreme Court forced the gender integration of the Virginia Military Institute (VMI) in the 1996 case *United States v. Virginia*. Until that time, Virginia did not permit women to enroll as cadets at VMI. Of course, opponents trotted out the usual arguments about the morality of men and women living in close quarters, the morale of the cadets, and the need to maintain an ordered and disciplined environment for the male population. The Court, however, decided that these justifications were insufficient to survive constitutional scrutiny and that the VMI policy violated the equal protection clause of the Fourteenth Amendment. A majority of the justices, including even Chief Justice Rehnquist, reasoned that a longstanding tradition of discriminating against women was in no way a justification for compounding that unfortunate historical error by perpetuating it.

The institutionalized bigotry of the armed forces is not about to lose more ground by giving in on the gay issue. The "we have traditionally discriminated, so let's keep on doing it" argument certainly did not die with the VMI case. Justice Scalia, in a scathing dissent, had this to say: "Longstanding national traditions [are] the primary determinant of what the Constitution means . . . 'when a practice not expressly prohibited by the text of the Bill of Rights bears the endorsement of a long tradition of open, widespread, and unchallenged use that dates back to the beginning of the Republic, we have no proper basis for striking it down.'"[19] Basically he is saying that if we have always discriminated, there is no reason, at least no constitutionally mandated reason, to stop—unless the Constitution were specifically to say, "Women must be allowed entrance to any public educational institution," or "Gays must be allowed to serve in the nation's armed forces." Scalia's argument is comfortable for him and for most other bigots, because he, and they, know full well that the Constitution makes no such explicit guarantees. Of course, it is important to realize that, if such reasoning predominated, not only would homosexual equality be impossible, but most of the significant social advances of the last century, like the advancement of woman's rights or racial desegregation, never would have come to pass. Scalia's argument is a variation of the popular argument that because differences traditionally have been observed—that is the difference in men and women and gays and straights have traditionally been observed (and manipulated to leave one or the other group politically powerless)— we should go right on exaggerating those differences for no better reason than because it always has been that way.

The ban on gays in the military is little more than an extended manifestation of this irrationality. It is a defensive action on the part of the insecure person—in the case of opposition to women or gays in the military, the straight male, who sees his masculinity threatened if women and gays assume a position of equality with him. If they rise from their traditional positions of weakness to a place on par with him, he thinks that his own strength is somehow diminished. The woman and the gay man have, in the eyes of the straight male bigot, a very close commonality: they are *pansies*— dainty, weak, and trivial. And he would just as soon keep them that way. When the woman or the gay man is a warrior of equal prowess, for whom is the straight man to puff out his chest? Who will validate his feelings of superiority? His relevance, as he sees it, is diminished.

This passing of straight male hegemony in yet another aspect of society is assuredly the reason for the strong resistance to the integration of gays into the military. Moral reasons can be, and routinely have been, proffered, but bigotry has little to do with morality. If it were really a question of morality, as the ban supporters suggest, wouldn't they be equally, if not more, concerned over the violation of the rights of women in the military? Why did comparable outrage not burst from the mouths of every serviceman in the wake of the Tailhook scandal? The results of a Department of Defense study, leaked to the press, showed that almost a quarter of the female cadets that graduated from the U.S. Military Academy in 2003 had been sexually assaulted during their matriculation at the academy. The primary reasons given by the cadets for not reporting the abuse were fear of ostracism by peers and fear of punishment. If sexual morality is an honest concern for the average serviceman, or of his administrators, why does the sexual violation of women continue to occur in the military and its schools?

Perhaps it is because the kind of man who fears being sexually desired or subjugated by the gay man in his communal shower is the kind of man who would affirm his own masculinity by forcing himself on a woman who did not invite him. Perhaps the greatest fear of the protestors of military integration of gays is the fear that the treatment they have reserved for women will be visited upon them. Such fears are, of course, unfounded. As Barry Goldwater commented in the *Washington Post* and *Los Angeles Times,* "[G]ays have served honorably in the military since at least the time of Julius Caesar. They'll still be serving long after we're all dead and buried."[20] Goldwater also pointed out that a study conducted by the navy in 1956 (although never made public) found gays to be good security risks. After all, who is better at being covert and guarding secrets—the straight man whose world falls apart at the thought of sharing a shower with a gay man, or the gay man who serves honorably, all the while secreting a defining part of himself?

The position of the U.S. government on the issue is such an absurd contradiction that it borders on the grotesque. In 1987, during the Reagan administration, a group of military personnel sued the U.S. government when they realized they had been the subjects of certain experimental testing without their knowledge or consent. The government successfully argued that soldiers give up their rights to privacy, even to bodily autonomy, when they enter the military and that neither their knowledge nor their consent was necessary for the government to use them as guinea pigs.[21] Today, the government argues that if gays were allowed in the military, straight soldiers would lose the freedom of association that they enjoy in civilian life. The inconsistency between a position that would have a soldier enjoy such a diminished right to privacy that he could be made the subject of secret, dangerous testing without his knowledge or consent and a position that worries about the compromise of the soldier's freedom of association if he is forced to share barracks with a gay soldier, is staggering.

Such perverse argumentation is seemingly endless. Behind it all we see not a legitimate concern for morality, security, morale, or privacy, but an irrational contempt for the homosexual as a person. We see, then, that the issues of gays or women in the military were never about gays or women per se. Instead they are about the sexually insecure heterosexual male and the shattering of the illusion of his own masculinity when he is forced to serve alongside a gay man or a woman as his equal.

I have no problem with the equation of gays with pansies: We are beau-

tiful and we are tough. The military needs us. It needs the tenacity of a people who have been kicked in the teeth more times than history can record
and have arisen and gone on. It needs the loyalty of a people who have been
disenfranchised and yet desire to serve a country that has not always served
them. An August 2003 Fox News poll revealed that 64 percent of Americans favored allowing gays to serve openly in the armed forces (a Gallup
Poll of the same year put the number at an even larger 80 percent), a significant increase from the numbers in a similar 2001 poll.[22] Perhaps, in our
need for a heightened state of readiness after 9/11, Americans are realizing
that prejudice is insidious and destructive and that it undermines the effec-
tiveness of all that it touches. Prejudice against gays is undermining the ef-
fectiveness and integrity of America's military. The ultimate panacea for
that and for any prejudice is the truth—and exposure to the truth.

But, as the earlier example of the gay business professor illustrated, heterosociety does not bear the whole blame for the closet. It may have been
constructed by heterosociety, or because of it, but there is an element of
fault in the gay community as well. In America today, increasing importance is placed on being out or in. It is a sign of our progress that more and
more gay people feel comfortable openly sharing their sexuality. Not all
gays, however, see this as positive. Prominent social critic and gay author
Bruce Bawer, for example, has written that he has not always been forth-
coming about his sexuality because it "seemed to [him] that the very act of
staging such a scene [coming out] constituted an announcement that sexual orientation is a Big Deal."[23] I understand Bawer's point that being gay
shouldn't be a big deal. But the fact remains that being gay in America
today *is* a very big deal, even if it is becoming mercifully less so, because
there are still enough bigots to *make* it a big deal for a great many people.

The bigot is aided in his endeavors by the emergence of a gay right that
negatively views gay activism and seeks to marginalize all gays who do not
fit within its highly restrictive definition of acceptability (read: heteroconformity). For example, when I read and reread Bawer's acclaimed *A Place at
the Table* (I really did approach the book with a tenacious determination to
like it—though in the end I could not), I discovered that Bawer strikes at
practically every aspect of gay culture that deviates from straight society's
model. I was amazed at his barely contained vitriol for nonmainstream
(read: effeminate or gay-acting) gays. In one representative passage he
writes, "I've talked to men who say that they knew they were gay when they
were as young as six or seven. In my experience, such men tend to have

been 'sissy boys' who always identified with women rather than men, whose difference from other boys was manifest in their childhood not only to themselves, but to others, and who as teenagers longed for older, more masculine men to take care of them—a longing that I have never experienced."[24] Gay conservatives attack effeminate gays, drag queens, transgenders, or anyone else they can label as "other" so as to distance themselves from the prevalent aspects of the gay community that would, by mere identification, make them less straight-acting. Bawer and those like him will mock the drag queen, will blame the drag queen for antigay prejudice because of his "weirdness." They are disdainful of overtly gay-acting individuals. Indeed, they would admonish those courageous and open individuals to censor themselves so as not to offend the otherwise sympathetic majority.

This is an uncommonly silly argument, for it turns the hateful structure of the closet upside down, and those embarrassing gays who cannot be pushed back inside it are simply smashed beneath it. Curiously, the burden of the closet is not placed on those gays who remain closeted and thereby deprive the gay community of their voices for change or even on the public figures employing the monstrous mechanism of the closet to enforce ages-old inequities. Instead, blame is placed on the gay individual who is very open about his sexuality and who has shown tremendous courage in doing what many in the gay right have not managed to do—live honestly. Much of their work is rife with playground name-calling and is as pointedly salacious as (allegedly) are the lives of those gays they scorn. Essentially, they merely perpetuate the heterosexist system of rewarding those gays who indulge their homosexuality clandestinely, ensuring that the ages-old gender conventions remain intact. These gay conservatives see themselves in a class with so-called normal men, somewhere across the imaginary line that separates the normal men from the faggots.

Despite the contentions of the gay conservatives, coming out isn't a validation of the bigots' prejudices; rather, it is an assertion that their prejudices will not force us to hide or to live our lives under false pretenses. Bawer views with disdain events like National Coming Out Day. He calls it "a manifestation of the subculture's failure to recognize that coming out is not a one-day event but an ongoing process, and that it should begin not when some subculture-designed calendar says it should but when the individual in question is psychologically, socially, and financially prepared to face the consequences."[25] Again, I agree with Bawer's plain wisdom, but he misses the point about gay pride events like Coming Out Day: They send a message to the young man in rural North Carolina struggling to find the words to tell his family or his classmates, or to the Manhattan executive in his fifth decade struggling to tell his colleagues, that he is not alone. That is hugely important. If struggling with one's sexual identity is a painful, wounding experience, believing that one is alone in the struggle is the unnecessary salt poured into the wound.

If coming out is important for many gays, it is equally important for our straight brothers and sisters. In 1986, the U.S. Supreme Court chose to uphold Georgia's dignity-robbing sodomy laws. In the case of *Bowers v. Hardwick*, the Court was presented with the question whether the federal Constitution's guarantees of privacy forbade the government from entering one's home and arresting one for consensual sex acts being performed in private with a member of the same sex. Instead of addressing this question— which it could only, with principle, have answered "yes"—the Court recast the question as whether there is a fundamental right to engage in homosexual sodomy. This was particularly insulting, because Georgia's law, as written, applied to both homosexual and heterosexual acts of sodomy, and in the case of petitioner Hardwick, oral sex. The opinion of the Court was clearly an expression of antigay bias, and it was recognized as such by the Court in 2003, when the decision was overruled in *Lawrence v. Texas.*

Justice Powell was the swing vote in *Bowers v. Hardwick.* Powell didn't join the ridiculously reasoned majority opinion or the uncommonly hateful concurring opinion of Chief Justice Burger. Instead, he filed his own concurring opinion in which he said that if petitioner Hardwick had been imprisoned, Georgia's law might have violated the Eighth Amendment's prohibition against cruel and unusual (read: excessive) punishment.

Interestingly, Justice Powell later said his vote had been a mistake and that he should have voted with the wing of the Court wishing to strike down antigay laws. What is most extraordinary, however, is the report that during the deliberation of the case, Powell said to one of his clerks that the justice was more than seventy years old and had never actually met a gay person. Ironically, the clerk to whom Powell confided this delicacy was himself gay.[26]

Powell's belief that he had never met a gay person seems to be consistent with the beliefs of many Americans at the time. A 1985 Gallup Poll found that only one in five Americans reported having a gay acquaintance. But when one considers that Alfred Kinsey's sex studies published in 1948 and

1953 had determined that 4 percent of the population were exclusively homosexual in their sex practices, another 5 percent had virtually no heterosexual experience, and nearly 20 percent had at least as many homosexual as heterosexual experiences, Powell's statement and the Gallup Poll seem extraordinary.[27] Since Kinsey's study, scientific speculations about the number of homosexuals in the country have held relatively constant, hovering around 10 percent, as Kinsey indicated.

Today, of course, fewer people could honestly make Powell's assertion, and fewer would be likely to cast their vote in keeping with the 1985 consensus of the Gallup Poll. Homosexuals are much more visible members of society in the twenty-first century than they were even in the late twentieth century. Yet the fact remains that if Kinsey's studies are reliable, if the general consensus about the number of homosexual individuals living in this country is true, much more can be said than that more people simply "know" a homosexual person. As Richard Mohr asserts in his 1988 work, *Gays/Justice: A Study of Ethics, Society, and Law,* two out of every five men one passes on the street have had orgasmic sex experiences with men; one out of every two families in the United States has a homosexual member; and many more people have homosexual experiences to one or another degree of frequency.[28] Gay men and women are everywhere in our society, and, despite the recent surge in coming out experiences, many of them are unknown to the people nearest them, to the people with whom they come in contact every day. That fact has made coming out a very visible action by the men and women who courageously do so, often making it the central moment of the gay experience for gays and nongays alike. Existing in the closet—hiding one's true self—is the predominant characteristic of gay life in the United States; otherwise, coming out would not be invested with such monumental status.

The ignorance that follows from lack of personal knowledge is pervasive. On a September 9, 2003, broadcast of *Larry King Live*, radio evangelist and fundamentalist religious pundit James Dobson asserted, "I don't believe that most homosexuals really want to marry." I couldn't help wondering how many homosexuals he had asked. In that same program, Dobson, of course, dismissed the Kinsey studies as "fraud."

I don't mean, in any way, to assert that Dobson speaks for most Americans. Dobson's is an exaggerated, volitional ignorance. But statements like Dobson's underscore the danger of making assumptions about gays without actually knowing gay people. Lack of knowledge feeds dangerous myths: the idea that all gays are sex-crazed maniacs, for example, or the overwhelming association of pederasty with homosexuality. All child abuse is horrific; the idea that abuse is made worse by the sexual orientation of the person perpetrating it is more than difficult to understand. Nonetheless, when a case of a gay individual sexually assaulting a child is reported, generalizations immediately are made that the proclivity to sexually molest children is somehow inherent in the gay person's makeup.

We saw this kind of deranged thinking in the Catholic Church abuse scandal. Circumstances, studies, and testimony were ignored, and priests abusing young boys were immediately pronounced "homosexual" whether or not there was any evidence that the men perpetrating the abuse were gay. Somehow, pedophilia became synonymous with homosexuality, although studies show that the majority of pedophiles are heterosexual men. Conversely, when incidents of heterosexual child abuse are reported, no one makes the assertion that the proclivity to sexually abuse is an inherent trait in all heterosexuals. Such wild and harmful suppositions directed at gays are a direct result of the knowledge void that separates many gays from much of heterosexual society.

WHY COME OUT?

It should be obvious that establishing a common humanity with heterosociety is of vital importance for gay rights. I have come to the conclusion that, as much as he professes to be bothered by stereotypical gays—men with limp wrists who sway when they walk and refer to each other as "girl"—the bigot is really much more uncomfortable with assimilationist or straight-acting gays. The stereotypical gay man is easy to spot at a hundred yards; he can be isolated, ghettoized, and easily identified as aberrant. The ease with which this individual can be labeled and identified is exactly what the bigot wants. What frightens him most is the gay man who plays tennis at the country club, plays guard on the soccer team, or showers at the gym: the undetected presence that can be neither labeled nor isolated, because he is exactly like his straight counterpart—except, of course, that he is sexually attracted to other men.

Coming out is, therefore, an important way to show heterosociety that gays are just like straight people in many ways. We are doctors, lawyers, teachers, neighbors, friends, and family. As Bawer himself has written, "Homophobia will not end until every heterosexual knows and cares about one gay person."[29] All the wisdom of the gay rights movement is summed up in those few words. A March 2004 *Los Angeles Times* poll showed a sharp disparity between the attitudes toward gays of the youngest and oldest generations of Americans. Americans eighteen to twenty-nine stated that they knew someone who was gay. Their responsiveness to the equal humanity of gays was more positive than that of people in the sixty-five and over category, in which only a bare majority knew a gay person. Nearly a decade before, a 1985 *Times* poll showed that more than half of U.S. residents did not know anyone who was gay. With this increased awareness, a correlative shift in attitudes is also perceptible. In a *Times* survey taken in 1983, 38 percent of the respondents said that they were sometimes or always uncomfortable around gays. A June 2000 survey found that the number had dropped to 29 percent. Even a plurality of the religious right said that they are fine with being around gay people today. In fact, in the 2004 *Times* survey the religious right were eight percentage points more likely to support gay rights if they knew a gay person than if they did not. They were ten points more likely to be sympathetic and eleven points less likely to be concerned about the orientation of a child's playmate's parent. Significantly, the religious right were nineteen points more likely to believe that a gay person could be a good role model if they knew a gay person than if they did not.[30]

Coming out, then, although an intensely individual experience, has societal ramifications and effects that we cannot always foresee. Many closeted gays and gay-friendly individuals see things from their own safe distances and gather strength and understanding from observing the out gay man or woman living his or her everyday life. Thus it is paramount that we make ourselves known and accessible.

Arguments about the importance and efficacy of coming out of the closet herald a fundamental discordance within the gay community. This cacophony centers on just what the movement should be about and in what direction it should proceed. Gays are still asking the questions that the Mattachine Society began asking more than fifty years ago: "Who are we?" "Where do we come from?" "What are we here for?" These remain the crucial questions today, for the more advancement enjoyed by gay people, the greater the danger that their inspiritment and motivation to carry on will falter. There is perhaps no more important contemporary debate within the gay community than that between groups I will call the assimilationists and the integrationists.

The crux of the assimilationist argument is, at first blush, a very tenable presumption—that gays aren't really that different from straights. They posit that because heterosociety is dominant, the aim of the gay rights movement is to capitalize on our similarities in order to conform as closely as possible to the hetero template. The assimilationists are gaining ground. Basically they put forth the proposition that gay people, save for their sexual orientation, are no different from heterosexuals. This statement seems perfectly acceptable, indeed, even highly desirable. But there is a problem: For the assimilationist, inclusion in heterosociety is a panacea. Yet it should be clear to even the mean student of history that inclusion in heterosociety without some consideration of our differences, real or imagined, is rife with potential problems. As James Baldwin warned, when a minority group attempts to assimilate, it usually does so entirely on the terms of the majority, dominant society. Baldwin's point is that a minority politics that panders to the same predominating majoritarian values that have held the minority in bondage can never realistically expect to achieve equality, let alone dignity, for the members of that minority. Gay people cannot afford—are not at a place in their civil rights movement—to assert simply, "We're no different than you; we're people too: Accept us." That course of action might yield some acceptance, but only for the gay person who fits the heterocentric definition of personhood—gay people who look, think, and behave as heterosociety thinks they should. This is a sacrifice the gay movement cannot afford to make; it is a sacrifice too heavy to be borne.

Success for the gay assimilationist is achieved by being as straight as possible. This is the goal of gays who brand every unconformity to the hetero paradigm as subculture. "Too gay" realities are branded subculture for a reason—to show their inferiority to the straight model. Any activity creating waves in the placid sea of straightness is avoided. An unfortunate byproduct is that assimilationists tend to blame nonassimilating gays for discrimination and inequality. But how, I ask, does the inability of the assimilationists to relate to the sissy boy make the sissy boy's self-awareness and self-discovery any less valid? How does it serve the cause to rob him of his deserved place, a place equal to that of assimilating gays, in society? Many assimilationists might be said to have it comparatively easy. They can be silent assimilators; when it becomes uncomfortable to be gay, they can simply pretend that they are other than they really are. But their pretending, in the long run, does little to make their lives or the lives of their brothers and sisters any better. Rather than fostering understanding, they merely hide themselves, along with whatever useful voice they might have. To- gether with Dr. King's dismay at those who sought to bargain with the American black by conceding some token measure of freedom in exchange for the black person's quietude and patience, I add my sad amazement at those gays who have bought the same old line. I maintain that a minority should not, indeed cannot, sacrifice its individuality for equality.

My personal opposition notwithstanding, I can understand the assimila- tionists' concerns. The differences between gays and straights have been ex- aggerated to the detriment of gays to keep them on the periphery. This has been clearly evidenced by the portrayal of gays on television. Although I acknowledge that visibility is important in any movement for equality, the *kind* of visibility we are afforded is also important.

Many of my friends lament the character of Jack on the NBC sitcom, *Will and Grace,* and admittedly, Jack is the personification of the gay stereo- type. He is effeminate, vain, shallow, sex-obsessed, hopelessly concerned with absolutely nothing that matters, and he is, at all times, the butt of everyone's joke. Unlike many of my friends, I see nothing wrong with the portrayal of an extremely effeminate gay man on television. In practically every community where there is a gay population there is a Jack. People should feel free to be who they are and, perhaps more important, who they want to be. After all, *Will and Grace* also has the Will character, who pres- ents a stable, successful, and masculine counter to Jack's outlandishness. Like it or not, both are part of our community; personally, I do like it.

But I join in the concern that the predominant media trend is to portray gays as foolish outsiders whose problems and lives are all trivial and laugh- able. I do not watch much television, and when I do turn it on, it certainly is not to a program that caters to the lowest common denominator, the rankest of the rank being the reality show. But when I heard about the Bravo network's new twist on the *Bachelor,* the dating reality show *Boy Meets Boy,* in which a gay man picks a potential mate from a pool of can- didates, I had to see for myself. Apart from the revulsion I feel for so-called reality programming, I was appalled to learn that the producers had mixed straight men into the dating pool. The real kicker was not that a gay man has been inserted into the *Bachelor* template, but that this gay man faced re- jection and humiliation because he could potentially pick a man com- pletely uninterested in a same-sex relationship with anyone.

Why this particular tag to the show? The answer is that the producers of the show were simply reinforcing what (they assumed) audiences wanted to

hear: Gay relationships are trivial and meaningless. So it is perfectly fine to
play with a gay man's emotions by allowing him to choose a partner that the
omniscient audience knows will have absolutely no interest in him.

It's a harmless, hardy laugh, right? Wrong—it's cruel.

The young woman picking her life mate on the *Bachelor* didn't have to
face the possibility that the man she chose would be gay and, therefore,
would reject her on national television. The message is explicit: gay reality
is one of practical joking at the gay man's expense, one that underscores his
inevitable sadness and loneliness. As Hutton Hayes adroitly put it in an article for the Advocate.com:

> The fool is never a threat, except to himself; he is merely laughable,
> the object of derision and contempt. Just as the depiction of the Jews
> as Shylock and the depiction of African Americans as Aunt Jemima
> ostensibly allowed those "outsiders" entry to the mainstream—in
> both instances only to allow the audience to laugh at them, rather
> than sympathize with them—so does the gay man as fool seemingly
> gain entry to the mainstream, only to find that since he is mocked he
> must remain an outsider.[31]

Certainly, not every Jew is spiteful, nor is every African American servile
and ignorant. So, too, not every gay person is trivial and aimless.

Likewise, the reducibility of everything gay to meaningless sex is undeniably a part of the mainstreaming of gays into society. But it is precisely the
thing that keeps gays set apart. I remember watching an episode of the show
Queer as Folk, filled with leather fetishists and man/boy love. A straight
friend turned to me and asked, "Is it really that way?" For some people, for
a very limited number, sure it is. But it isn't that way for most of the gay
people I know, and, I dare say, not for most of the gay people in *Queer as
Folk's* alleged setting, Pittsburgh. This is particularly disappointing when
the show comes from openly gay producers.

But the danger of the pervasive portrayal of gays with a singular, banal
definition as sexual maniacs, with tritely solved problems, and the perpetuated outsider status that assimilationists guard against is equaled in danger
by the assimilationists' desire to suppress any demonstrative difference
which does not fit their definition (read: heterosociety's definition) of normal or mainstream. "Trust thyself," wrote Ralph Waldo Emerson in his
Self-Reliance. "Insist on yourself. Never imitate." For Emerson, the self-

actualization that comes with trusting oneself was the golden promise of America. For eons, women and men had been forced to bend their wills and personalities to the whim of senseless authority, their behavior being the product of commandment and tradition. Emerson believed America to be something different; he believed it to be a place where conformity wasn't forced upon the individual by oppressive authority. "Whosoever would be a man," he declared, "must be a nonconformist."[32] Fully aware that it is a curious tightrope walk that allows for the creation of a meaningful culture for ourselves out of the shadows of rigid heteroconformity and also the achievement of recognition and acceptance within the panoply of society, I maintain that there is a feasible alternative to assimilation. The alternative is that which I would call integration.

Over the years, being gay has become ripe with a host of meanings that far outreach the mere physicality of sexual inclination. To be gay is to share with other gays a variety of religious, political, and social activities that truly constitute a gay community. That anthropological result of centuries of persecution needn't immediately subordinate itself to heterosociety: The gay community is a community every bit as concrete and meaningful as any heterosexual community. As author and activist Dennis Altman opined, "[A] gay cultural perspective should be one that never denies or hides homosexuality but that uses the experience of homosexuality to illuminate larger questions of the human condition."[33]

Of course, Altman also warned against a community that becomes too inward looking. We must resist the pigeonholing of our books as gay books, or our films as gay films, or even our politics as gay politics. We should also, I contend, resist the temptation simply to make our books, and films, and politics the books, and films, and politics of heterosociety. We need not and should not assimilate only on the terms of the dominant majority society. In sum, everything we are need not be gay but we should not hide or smother those parts of us that *are* gay. By asking its questions, the Mattachine Society sought to understand gay oppression rather than to hide from it or hope it out of existence. The years that followed Stonewall showed a calculated combination of gay politics and culture aimed at the upward mobility of gays within American society. Gays weighed and often rejected the religious, political, and social constructs of heterosociety as unsuited for the fulfillment of the whole gay person. Therefore, new religious, political, and social construction was a necessity.

If one believes that the only differences between gays and straights are differences in sexual inclination, perhaps assimilation would represent a suitable tool for societal vindication and individual well-being. I, however, am not convinced that such assimilation is possible. Gays might themselves recognize that their personhood is composed of far more than their sexual orientation, but much of the larger society does not. Despite what gays might do to downplay the connotation, many straights will continue to see gays only in terms of sexuality. The fear and hatred of sex is so pervasive in this country, stemming as it does from a puritanical social morality compounded over the centuries, that no matter what portions of gay communal identity gays renounced in order to assimilate comfortably into the heterosexual paradigm, it would likely never be enough. Homosexuality is the antithesis of most of what Western culture has to say about sex and gender; it is the destruction of most of the patriarchical gender construction of the past two thousand years. Under the assimilationist postulation, society may, indeed, move toward a toleration of some gays, those who can easily pass as the straight model, but it would always be only a partial, begrudging acceptance.

Thus, one might conclude—certainly the assimilationist might—that the closet remains significant in our lives, not because it changes us fundamentally but because it is the most convenient tried-and-true way of accomplishing tasks and contending with attitudes that cannot be accomplished or attended to by other means. These are ultimately the concerns of self-maintenance, preserving both private and public life with as few scrapes and bruises as possible. But truly living is about more than mere self-preservation; it is about cultivating the best within us and resisting the worst. It always requires a keen understanding of who we are, where we come from, and what we are here for. This is what the closet has stolen from us. This is the reason that living in the closet, even the modified version that assimilationists tout, is an unconscionable way to go on living in the United States of America. It should be the aim of every principled gay individual to secure the inclusion in society of every other gay person, not just the straight-looking or straight-acting gay person. Only then can we optimistically look for the total obliteration of the closet. It is a work both necessary and good.

CHAPTER 2

"Through a Glass Darkly"

American Religious Fundamentalism and Homophobia

Our moral mentors told us it was an age of unprecedented license and corruption, and that we boys and girls who had just cracked our shells were a brood of vipers from the pit.

—Elmer Davis

We have just enough religion to make us hate, but not enough to make us love one another.

—Jonathan Swift

ONE CANNOT DISCUSS THE PLACE OF THE GAY individual in American society without also discussing the American fundamentalist[1] religious phenomenon that has done much to shape gay life and to keep the progression of gay rights in America noticeably more limited than the progression of such rights in most of the remaining democratic West. Much of what must be said is not good. While writing this chapter, I told a friend "The irony is that people will read this and call me antireligious." Nothing could be further from the truth. I am a Christian, a convert to Catholicism, which in many ways still informs my worldview.[2] Just a few years ago, I wouldn't have considered writing a book about homosexuality or gay culture, let alone a book critical of the church. But I became acquainted with some young gay men who changed my mind. These young men were angry, and they had every right to be. What troubled me most was that their ire was directed heavily toward the Christian church.

It was no wonder, for at the time the Catholic Church's sexual abuse scandal had just broken, and the church did something quite predictable: It made the gay man its scapegoat, while ignoring its own immorality and mismanagement. Concerned, I wrote the following letter to William Curlin, then bishop of the diocese of Charlotte (my home diocese in North Carolina).

The Most Reverend and Dear Sir:

I am writing because I am concerned about some remarks made by high-ranking Catholic officials, including Bishop Wilton Gregory, in the wake of the recent child victimization issues facing our Church. Several statements have been made by those purporting to speak for the Church, which can be reduced to a latent bigotry against homosexuals. . . . [I]t seems that bringing homosexuals into the forefront of the crisis as a scapegoat can serve only to introduce a further point of divisiveness, a course of conduct wholly beneath the dignity of the Church.

I believe that the inquiry should be the same for all priests: (1) Do they take seriously the vows by which they committed their lives to the Lord's service? and (2) Are they good and effective priests? Casting the blame for the actions of individuals on a whole class of people doesn't seem to serve either of these inquiries; and resorting to such a jejune explanation for what has occurred within the Church can only serve to work an injustice on homosexuals who faithfully serve the Church and who turn to it for spiritual guidance.

Even as we face allegations of abuse in our own diocese, I hope that you will strive to focus attention where it is needed and to make certain that the horrific events of late do not serve to create further prejudice against homosexuals, a group already marginalized and facing insolence within the Church.

I received no response from Bishop Curlin, and the Catholic Church did what I feared it would do: The church sought to ban homosexuals from the priesthood, to make it more difficult for them to conscientiously enroll in seminaries.

Nearly a year later, I was at a conference in Seattle and I had occasion to visit the impressive cathedral there. The mass was beautiful, and in the church's bookstore, I bought Cardinal Bernardin's *The Gift of Peace*. The book was eloquent and moving, telling of the cardinal's heartbreak at being falsely accused of abuse and of his reconciliation with his openly gay accuser. The U.S. Supreme Court only had recently handed down its decision in *Lawrence v. Texas*, the case that struck down the country's remaining sodomy laws as violative of a right to privacy under the federal Constitution. In the aftermath of that vindicating moment, my thoughts again turned to the church. I remembered then, as I do today, the tingles of validation, the little hairs on the back of my neck standing at attention when I read the *Lawrence* decision. In my hotel room that night, however, I felt only despair. I thought of the Anglican Church's trouble when it sought to appoint an openly gay church leader and I thought of the problems in my own church. I drafted the following letter to the archbishop of Atlanta, head of the province that encompasses the Carolinas and Georgia.

I write to express my concern about an issue of growing importance to the Roman Catholic Church and to the Christian community at large. Recently, as I am sure you are aware, the Church of England rescinded the impending appointment of an openly gay candidate for church leadership because of international conflict over the issue of homosexuality.

Some time ago, I wrote to Bishop Curlin of the Diocese of Charlotte expressing my fears that gay priests were being—and would continue to be—unfairly targeted after the break of the Church's abuse scandal and in the wake of the most unfortunate comments coming out of the National Conference of Catholic Bishops, specifically those of Bishop Wilton Gregory, equating the problem of pedophilia with homosexuality. My fears in that regard have not been assuaged.

Despite all these events on the national and international stage, what has most prompted this letter is my recent acquaintance with several homosexual men. They are only young adults, in their late teens and twenties (one of them a Catholic school student), but they are already so jaded by the Church's response to their sexual orientation that they have turned their backs on their Faith.

As a lawyer, the issue of equality for homosexuals began for me as a social issue. But coming to know these young men has lodged it as a permanent part of my everyday religious consciousness. The law, which consumes so much of my time, is, of course, imperfect, but the Christian church should be equally a refuge for all people. And yet somewhere between literalism and closed-mindedness we have lost the Gospels' basic message of humanity. Isn't it sad that in this the most generous nation on Earth, a young man, not very much older than those boys who mean so much to me, can be beaten and left to die, lashed to a crude fence in rural Wyoming—all because of a biological trait. I believe this is but a symptomatic expression of an underlying disease—a disease that I fear is being fed by religion itself.

Gays, I think it can be fairly said, remain the last minority against whom it is permissible to openly discriminate. We know, of course, that much of this comes from interpretations of the writings of St. Paul. I cannot dispute that he marked homosexuality as a seed of damnation. There are the endless disputes about the exact subject of his disapprobation. Some say it was the pagan temple practices prevalent in the gentile world with which St. Paul took issue. Whatever his reasons, we should not forget that St. Paul's words have been used to justify a host of historical ills: slavery, the subjugation of women, and so on. But while these issues have finally (arguably at least) found favorable resolution in the Church, gays have not been so fortunate.

The disease has spread and continues to spread. Consequently, gays are marginalized by the Church. Born free, as they are born in the image of God, they are held captive by violence and hypocrisy, expressions in the image of the world into which they were born, not of the Creator who gave them life. While others can look to the Church as a refuge in this harsh world, gays cannot; they are shoved into pariah castes and pushed outside of our churches, all on account of something it is becoming increasingly clear they cannot control. When we welcome them, we do so out of "charity," not out of unconditional love. In so doing, we trivialize their humanity, and accordingly our own. At bottom, we make them doubt whether they are loved by God, and that must be the greatest blasphemy of all; and it comes directly from the mouth of the Church—all this from a few words in St. Paul's letters in the New Testament.

We should also be careful not to forget that St. Paul was writing to a very different people at a very different time; and St. Paul, unlike the God who inspired him, was not infallible. As the Church has, implicitly at least, recognized his human error in judgment about slaves and women, it should also acknowledge his error about gays.

The germane question is whether he would write the same message to us today. I think he would not. St. Paul's very estimable life, after all, was devoted to sharing what had begun as a gift for a select few (the Jews) with a great many (the rest of the human family); he brought Christ's gospel to the gentiles. Excluding any group on account not of a choice, but of a biological determinant is completely out of sync with that message. Jesus, himself, emphasized love at the price of exclusion:

> You shall love the Lord your God with all your heart, with all your soul, and with all your mind . . . you shall love your neighbor as yourself. On these two commandments hang all the Law and all the Prophets.

If literal interpretation is to be the rule in this issue, why then are these words not the final recourse of the Church.

In my opinion, what made Jesus, as a pastor, so genuine and authentic was his constant presence with the people. He actively sought out the lost sheep. By merely being accessible, Jesus allowed the people to experience the salvation of God in some way: to be healed of their sicknesses, to be fed with the Scriptures, or simply to have their questions answered. Surely this tradition of bringing the living God to the people is the continuing mission of the Church—a mission that, detached from any segment of the people, we cannot fulfill.

Archbishop, I beg your pardon in my being so bold as to offer education in matters of Faith. But I feel that it is imperative that we move beyond our distrust and polarization about this issue at every level, because entrenchment hampers our ministry to a segment of our human family. I am confident that we will eventually see intolerance change to inclusiveness. Christianity, like anything true that endures, is only fully realized in time—a little more fully as the world grows older. In the meantime, when I am confronted by young gay men who have turned their backs on God because of the reaction of their churches, I am moved to urgency in my hope that the Church will sooner than later place itself on the right side of history.

I pray that you will keep my reservations in mind as you and the other bishops plan the future of the Church in the United States.

Again, there was no response, but by this point, my focus, at least insofar as gay rights were concerned, was clear. I had to work out the place of the gay individual in American society, and that place was intertwined inextricably with religious attitudes and prejudices that inform the American consciousness in matters from personal morality to law and back again. My letter to the archbishop had touched upon what I believe to be the biggest threat to the welfare of the gay individual in the United States: homophobia.

There is much about our American quasi theocracy that should give the gay individual pause. In response to the 1986 U.S. Supreme Court decision in *Bowers v. Hardwick,* the infamous case that upheld the criminalization of consensual gay sex acts, Richard Posner, a federal judge and law professor made the following comment in his book *Sex and Reason:*

> Statutes which criminalize homosexual behavior express an **irrational fear and loathing** of a group that has been subjected to discrimination, much like that directed against the Jews, with whom indeed homosexuals—who, like Jews, **are despised more for who they are than for what they do**—were frequently bracketed in medieval persecutions. The statutes thus have a quality of invidiousness missing from statutes prohibiting abortion or contraception. The position of the homosexual is difficult at best, even in a tolerant society, which our society is not quite; and it is made worse, though probably not much worse, by statutes that condemn the homosexual's characteristic methods of sexual expression as vile crimes . . . There is a gratuitousness, an egregiousness, a cruelty, and a meanness about [such laws]. (emphasis mine)[3]

Truly, in a world of irrational hatred and prejudice, the irrational hatred of homosexuals—homophobia—is a prejudice in a class by itself. Homosexuals remain the only minority against whom it is permissible to discriminate openly. Harvard professor (and Baptist minister) Peter Gomes is often quoted as saying that homophobia is "the last respectable prejudice of the century."[4] A comment made in the twentieth century, it remains no less true today. Moreover, homophobia is the only prejudice whose perpetrators routinely refuse to acknowledge it as such. They accomplish this in several ways. One way is to deny the biology of being gay. Blacks, the homophobe will argue, have not chosen to be black, but gays make the conscious choice to sleep with members of their own sex. The homophobe rationalizes that being gay is a lifestyle choice; thus, he is merely registering his disapprobation of a volitional act. In an article about the effort to add the controversial Amendment 2 to the Colorado constitution to deprive gays of protection against discrimination, Robert Nagel wrote, "There is the obvious but important possibility that one can 'hate' an individual's behavior without hating the individual."[5] But people like Nagel miss the point: When the "behavior" is an intrinsic, inseparable part of the personhood of the individual, the "obvious but important possibility" quickly becomes an impossibility. It makes for creative escapist rhetoric to be sure; but, in reality, hating the homosexual simply because he is homosexual is no different than hating the black man simply because he is black. Nagel's comment evinces a fundamental misunderstanding shared by many people: homosexuality as a chosen behavior.

There is even some manifestation of this "choice" illogic among gays themselves. Of course, each member of a minority group, even a despised and vilified group, identifies with the group as a whole to a different degree. I have friends, the most secular of secular Jews, who will jump to the defense of another, more religiously inclined Jew, in a New York minute, because they feel a fierce identification with the group. Not so among many gays. Many gays who can assimilate into straight society do so quietly, often blaming prejudice against gays on obviously gay individuals, thereby becoming complicit in the prejudice themselves. It is a key component of their own identities with which they do not—or do not wish to—connect.

The refusal to recognize antigay discrimination as prejudice is not reserved exclusively for society's baser elements. The inability to call a spade a spade exists in its erudite circles as well. Religious liberties scholar and federal judge for the Tenth Circuit Court of Appeals, Michael McConnell, for example, refuses to see unequal treatment of homosexuals under the law as appropriately discussed in traditional terms of discrimination. Although McConnell concedes that there are legal problems with unequal treatment, he stresses that labels such as "bigotry" and "discriminat[ion]" are not fitting labels for the unequal treatment faced by homosexuals, because what is perceived as bigotry or prejudice by some is merely an acceptable, moral normative statement of religious belief by others. This is all the more bewildering because McConnell concedes that homosexuality is an immutable, nonvolitional orientation.[6]

The aforementioned Colorado Amendment 2 demonstrates how homophobia has infiltrated and still does infiltrate the American legal system. The cities of Aspen, Boulder, and Denver had included protection for homosexuals in their ordinances banning discrimination in housing, employment, education, and some other areas. In direct response, in 1992, a majority of Colorado voters adopted, in a statewide referendum, a proposed amendment—called Amendment 2—to the state constitution. Amendment 2 provided:

> No Protected Status Based on Homosexual, Lesbian, or Bisexual Orientation. Neither the state of Colorado, through any of its branches or departments, nor any of its agencies, political subdivisions, municipalities or school districts, shall enact, adopt, or enforce any statute, regulation, ordinance or policy whereby homosexual, lesbian or bisexual orientation, conduct, practices or relationships shall constitute or otherwise be the basis of or entitle any person or class of persons to have or claim any minority status, quota preferences, protected status or claim of discrimination. This Section of the Constitution shall be in all respects self-executing.[7]

Civil rights watch groups took the state of Colorado to court over the amendment, and the Colorado Supreme Court eventually determined that Amendment 2 violated the equal protection guarantees of the Fourteenth Amendment to the U.S. Constitution. Because a state cannot enact, even by altering its own state constitution, a law that conflicts with the federal Constitution, Amendment 2 fell. The U.S. Supreme Court, final interpreter of the federal Constitution, affirmed the judgment of the Colorado Supreme Court, in the case of *Romer v. Evans*, stating: "[Amendment 2 was] born of animosity toward [homosexuals]. 'If the constitutional conception of "equal protection of the laws" means anything, it must at the very least mean that a bare . . . desire to harm a politically unpopular group cannot constitute a *legitimate* governmental interest.'"[8]

What do movements, like the movement to add Amendment 2 to the Colorado constitution, mean for gays? Could comparable state and federal legislation arise today to threaten gays?

The sociopolitical position of gays changed with the advent of Bill Clinton's presidency. Among the religious right, fear of promised progay Clinton policies prompted Pat Buchanan to declare a "culture war" at the 1992 Republican National Convention. Although Clinton did not follow through with his much-discussed promise to lift the ban on gays in the military, he did much to benefit homosexuals. He signed executive orders granting protection from discrimination in federal employment and ending the routine denial of security clearances on the basis of sexual orientation alone. The Clinton policies were signposts heralding a change in society's feeling about gays. Indeed, it seems that a great deal of what Buchanan and other hatemongers feared has come to pass. Young gays today are growing up in an America hugely different from the America known by gay youth just a generation ago. When Clinton took office in 1993, television networks were censoring programs like *Ellen;* today gay programming abounds. Increasingly, gays are coming out of the closet and demanding the rights to which they are entitled and the equality they deserve. It is inarguable that social acceptance has grown exponentially. In June 2003, the Supreme Court handed down its decision in *Lawrence v. Texas,* reversing the abominable *Bowers v. Hardwick,* and affording gays the human dignity (at least a measure of it) guaranteed to them by the Constitution.

But the victory in *Lawrence* underscored how far gays have yet to go. Despite the move toward social acceptance, progress for gays is slow, victories hard-won. Indeed, the small advances of the gay rights movement have entrenched the recalcitrant religious right even more, spurring efforts toward a constitutional amendment to define marriage in such a way as to forever exclude gays. The "don't ask, don't tell" policy on gays in the military remains in place; indeed, there has been renewed talk of reinstating an all-out ban.

What feeds such a strong negative reaction? Why have fair policies regarding gays been so slow to materialize? What accounts for the prevalence of homophobia in the United States?

The answer to these questions, I think, is found in my earlier allusions: As Letha Scanzoni and Virginia Mollenkott, authors of *Is the Homosexual My Neighbor?* indicate, "There is little doubt that much of the current discrimination against homosexual women and men is rooted in and fostered by the antigay sentiments voiced by certain religious leaders."[9] The corruptive existence and influence of America's fundamentalist religious right is testament to the verity of that statement. The Christian fundamentalist's obsession with sex and his insistence on conformity with his own version of morality is a disturbing American phenomenon. In no other nation on Earth—at least among those nations loosely defined as Christian—does such a prevalent hatred for gays exist. For example, the United States and Turkey remain the only original members of NATO to retain a ban on gays serving in their militaries. In no other progressive nation must gays face the treatment that they face in the United States, the birthplace of democracy and equality. In Europe, for example, the tide flows in the opposite direction. More pointedly, the Netherlands became the first nation in the world to allow gays to legally marry.[10] In Paris, France, where I spend a great deal of time, gays are afforded a much greater measure of social integration. There are, of course, pockets of hatred, but they are the exception.

What is the marked difference between nations like France or the Netherlands and the United States? The Netherlands, like most of Europe, is largely a secular nation; there is no religious right to speak of. At least there is no fundamentalist Christian right. There is a growing Islamic population that increasingly threatens the rights of homosexuals and other groups. Although their perversity may stem from different historical figures, Jesus or Mohammed, both fundamentalist incarnations are equally perverse. They espouse a rigid legalism, rather than a doctrine of love. But fundamentalist Islam in the Netherlands lacks the power and political clout of its Christian counterpart in the United States. In the United States, we arguably enjoy a greater bounty of temporal freedoms than any society on Earth, but freedom in America's religious conscience lags far behind that of the rest of the Western world.

FUNDAMENTALISM AND
THE KNOWLEDGE VOID . . .

Is my thesis—that America's fundamentalist religious experience causes misunderstanding and ignorance, and ultimately homophobia—too sweeping? Consider for a moment a 1976 statement by former President Jimmy Carter: "[T]he issue of homosexuality always makes me nervous," he said. When pressed for a reason by his interviewer (interestingly, *Playboy* magazine), he explained that his anxiety over homosexuality stemmed from his lack of personal knowledge on the subject and from his Baptist faith. Carter didn't explicitly connect his lack of knowledge and his Baptist affiliation, but the corollary is certainly a fair inference to draw.

I can relate; I grew up as a Southern Baptist. Those words, however, encompass a myriad of caveats. To say that I was raised in the Southern Baptist church would be to somewhat overstate the experience. Certainly, my mother dropped me off at a local Baptist Sunday school and then returned to pick me up when the hour was done. But that, I think, stemmed more from the nagging of her mother, my grandmother, than from any abiding belief in the importance of my religious instruction. My grandmother perpetually spoke of the importance of my being in church. Even at a young age, I was outspoken and I remember my response: "It's only some old man asking 'Do you love God or do you love the devil?'" But a few years later, when I was thirteen, I began attending church services with my younger sister's nanny and her husband at a primitive Baptist church.

I must note that this wasn't a matter of coercion; something inside me compelled me to go. As a young child and adolescent, I had a deep sense of displacement and disconnection from the world around me. Something in those hours filled a need. But something about the experience was also unsettling. The sermons I heard were overwhelmingly condemnatory; there was no content of love to the message, except the love of Christ's sacrifice on the cross that could save a soul. And even this was spoken of in terms of the human being's undeserving state to receive Christ's love and the many, many things he could do to deprive himself of that love. The people at the church gave me a sense of belonging to something bigger than myself; but they left me with an increasing sense of disconnection from the world around me.

I was taught to scorn those who rejected the church's fundamentalist beliefs. Of course, I was told, "Love the sinner, hate the sin," but that invariably translated into loving from afar—avoiding and shunning those less righteous than the born again believers who would doubtless inherit God's kingdom. Almost as soon, and as passionately, as I felt I belonged, I knew deep in my conscience that I did not. I was even warned not to get "too smart" and lose sight of God's mandates, as though intellect and spirituality were mutually exclusive.

Years later, I have come to understand that the very evil these people sought to avoid was exactly what had taken them in. I don't mean to say that the people themselves were evil. I think most people end up as fundamentalist adherents because they are lonely, desperate, or searching in some way. But the religion they embrace, whatever their good intentions, is most assuredly evil, for it replaces Christ's central message of love with legalism, fear, and exclusion—and that is undeniably evil. It replaces reliance on the

intellect and reason with reliance on a salvation experience and with un-
questioning acceptance of God's revealed truth, meted out to the believer
by an ordained man of God. On homosexuality, of course, there is but one
possible position—homosexuals are sinful, and their activities are abominations before God.

For this book I interviewed a friend of mine—a fundamentalist, charis-
matic Christian, who is also a gay man. He told me about growing up in the
fundamentalist tradition as an independent Baptist (a member of a church
that follows basic Baptist tenets of once saved, always saved and believer
baptism but that does not affiliate itself with the Southern Baptist Convention, which is the largest Protestant denomination in our country). My
friend related the confusion he felt, indeed the horror, after hearing years of
antihomosexual sermons, of discovering his own sexuality. In his church, as
is common in the fundamentalist tradition, homosexuality is one of the sins
that could separate one eternally from the will of God—send one to hell. It
is common in the Protestant tradition to reject the Catholic hierarchy of
mortal and venial sins by asserting that all sins are the same, each an equal
affront to God. But homosexuality holds a special place in the fundamentalist Protestant tradition; it is the sin that gives one over to a "reprobate
mind"—as it was described in my friend's church—which is the point of no
return, the point at which one is bound for hell's fire. My friend related how
he made weekly trips to the altar at his church to pray that God would de-
liver him from his sin. Then, at age sixteen, came the moment when his
mother found a *Playgirl* magazine stuffed under his mattress. Still, years
later, he told me that he did not have words to articulate the look of "disgust and hatred" on her face. His father was physically abusive, which
should not be surprising in a belief system where parents, fueled by antigay
hatred in the name of religion, put their children in positions of horrific
physical and psychological torment in order to reform or to save them from
the "reprobate mind." Ultimately, my friend questioned his relationship
with God and dabbled in drugs and anonymous sex to drown his feelings of
self-hatred and lack of acceptance. He lied to his parents and told them that
God had "removed" his "sin."

What continues to astonish me most about my friend's experience, however, is the fact that my friend is still an active member of the same congregation in whose name he suffered such abuse. "It's just the way I feel."
He was adamant in this. At first, I was at a loss. "How you feel?" I asked,
disbelievingly. "How could one who heard on countless occasions sermons

denouncing an essential part of his being as reprobate and sinful feel that he belonged in such a fold?" I got only blank stares. He refused to entertain the slightest dissent on the doctrinal points that essentially damned him.

In the face of this inscrutability, I began to formulate an answer for myself. Fundamentalism depends upon a lack of questioning. Fundamentalists, after all, believe that they have a monopoly on revealed truth. That truth is doled out in fire and brimstone sermons as unshakable and unquestionable. If someone is foolish enough to question, he is immediately denounced as reprobate, and the challenge to the establishment is vehemently quelled. My friend, no doubt, had never challenged his belief system because he had feared to. Challenging the belief systems of our childhood can be a horrifying experience; rising above standards ingrained in us since childhood can be an enormous struggle. Moreover, he had been taught not to think about it. As Bruce Bawer put it in his book, *Stealing Jesus*, fundamentalism can be understood as a way of "avoiding the obligation to *think*—and, especially, to think for oneself." In that way, spiritually immature people mistake the voices of aggressive socialization for the voice of God.

The ranks of fundamentalist denominations are swelled by the undereducated, and the churches themselves teach a certain aversion to any education or philosophy that threatens their truth. To the extent that it is known in the rest of the world, fundamentalism's success is a direct corollary to its missionary work with the poor and uneducated. This aversion to knowledge of alternatives is a characteristic that fundamentalist Protestants share with reactionary Catholics, Jehovah's Witnesses, and Mormons, although more than one of these groups would no doubt question the Christianity of the others. The idea that it is part of man's natural evolution to question why he believes what he believes is their anathema. Knowledge is power, as the old adage goes, and it is a power that purveyors of fundamentalism do not want their proselytes to possess. They fear their treachery will be discovered. They fear that their dupe will discover that Jesus' death was not some sort of cosmic business deal by which sins were paid for and lives bought. The dupe may discover that, to the contrary, Christ's giving of his life was just that, a gift, the ultimate act of love and selflessness, freely offered to all people without prescription and without recipe.

They fear the dupe may discover that, rather than to bring more rules and legalism to Earth, Christ's main mission was to teach God's love and acceptance of every individual. The dupe may discover that Christ's love extends to all those he has banned from his life on account of race, creed, or sexual orientation—he may discover that we are all precious to our Creator, without resort to the law. He may discover that God loves more than those people who have been saved by following his guidelines.

The dupe may learn that rather than distrust his own intellectual inclinations, he should embrace them as the greatest gifts the Creator has given—the shortest path to actualization of Christ's love. He may discover that the truth is not held in monopoly by the born again, but that it is known fully only to God and that religious traditions merely point the way vaguely to something too wide and too vast to be expounded fully by any one religious incarnation.

He may learn that God is not an angry, fearsome, despotic God, but a God of love, unconditional and all-inclusive.

FUNDAMENTALISM AND THE DEMISE OF LIBERAL DEMOCRACY . . .

The danger that fundamentalism poses to democratic ideals and individual liberties is real. As an example, I share with the reader two quotes: (1)"The National Government will regard it as its first and foremost duty to revive in the nation the spirit of unity and cooperation. It will preserve and defend those basic principles on which our nation has been built. It regards Christianity as the foundation of our national morality, and the family as the basis of national life"; (2)"We must not allow our children and children's children to grow up in a nation with legalized polygamy, common law marriage and same-sex marriage. The only way to put the traditional and biblical family form of one man married to one woman safely out of the reach of future courts and legislatures is to pass an amendment to the U.S. Constitution."[11] Reading the quotes in tandem, the reader could easily believe that they were made by the same speaker. However, the first quote came from a 1933 speech delivered by Adolf Hitler; the other came from an American televangelist and political agitator, the Reverend Jerry Falwell. If not the product of the same speaker, these statements are most assuredly products of the same mind-set. Indeed, to the Christian fundamentalist represented by the likes of Falwell, except for the right to proselytize his particular brand of religion, individual civil liberties are seen as evil, as threats to fundamentalist survival. The fundamentalists have been masterful at spreading their ideas to America's citizenry; they have convinced many

Americans that the United States was founded on their particular brand of religious identity. Falwell, leader of the Moral Majority and the Liberty Federation, fundamentalist organizations that act like political action groups, has also said: "The Founders actually included their Christian beliefs in their Declaration of Independence." He went on to say that "[the Founders] believed in absolute truth which they called unalienable rights or self-evident truths. The Founders were men of the Bible. They considered this 'absolute Truth' . . . self-evident Truths."[12]

Likewise, James Dobson, founder of Focus on the Family, whose tirades against homosexuals are almost endless, has stated that "it is utterly foolish to deny that we have been, from the beginning, a people of faith whose government is built wholly on a Judeo-Christian foundation. Yet those of our people who do not study our history can be duped into anything." Of course, if Americans did study their own history, they easily would discover the duplicity inherent in most of what Dobson asserts about America's founding ideals. But he can make this statement, for he knows that his fundamentalist adherents aren't going to take up the challenge—they have been taught that questioning is wrong, even sinful. Pat Robertson, television evangelist and former presidential candidate, has said that our country was designed for "self-government by Christian people." These foolhardy suppositions aren't just the material of half-baked television evangelists; they have been swallowed by respected academics like Michael Novak, who has claimed that the God of the Declaration of Independence "is not, and cannot be, a remote watchmaker God." Indeed, Novak argues that, by choosing the words "Creator" and "Nature's God," Jefferson was making an effort to link the God of the Declaration of Independence to the God of the Bible. Former President George H. W. Bush has proclaimed that, unless a person believes in the God of the Declaration of Independence, he cannot be a true American. Former presidential candidate and U.S. Representative Alan Keyes has noted that the God of the Declaration is "a very biblical God." In 1999, John Ashcroft, speaking at Bob Jones University, told an assembly of graduates that America was founded on religious principles (he needn't specify which religion) and "we have no king but Jesus." Even Democratic presidential hopeful Joseph Lieberman, a Jew, has spouted the same nonsense about the Declaration's biblical links, though the Falwells and Robertsons of the world would likely not care to keep company with such a nonbeliever.[13]

This poison has affected Americans en masse. When Roy Moore, then chief justice of the Alabama Supreme Court, was ordered to remove a two-ton monument of the Ten Commandments (a monument Moore had placed there without authorization) from the Alabama supreme court building by a federal judge, who declared that the monument violated the Constitution's protections against government establishment of religion, fundamentalist supporters of Moore turned out in droves, threatening civil disobedience to make sure their precious monument was not removed. They believed—sincerely, I will admit—that such a monument was entirely in keeping with the principles upon which the United States was founded.

The power of the fundamentalists to speak louder and to have their ideas made law is astonishing. Consider, again, the case of *Bowers v. Hardwick*. Hardwick and his partner were arrested for violating Georgia's anti-sodomy law. A police officer was admitted by a friend to Hardwick's home in order to serve a warrant and found Hardwick and his partner having oral sex in the bedroom. Although the state decided not to proceed with the case, Hardwick, believing that his rights had been violated, pushed forward his claim for constitutional vindication. Ultimately, the case reached the U.S. Supreme Court. The resulting decision is one of the true travesties of American constitutional history and a glaring example of the dangerous and distorting influence of religious legalism on the United States' legal system.

In fact, the Court upheld the Georgia statute precisely because "[p]roscriptions against [homosexuality] have ancient roots." The "ancient roots" were undeniably religious roots, and the Court made no effort to assert otherwise. Chief Justice Burger wrote a concurring opinion to underscore the fact: "Condemnation of [homosexual] practices is firmly rooted in Judeo-Christian moral and ethical standards . . . During the English Reformation when powers of the ecclesiastical courts were transferred to the King's Courts, the first English statute criminalizing sodomy was passed." As Justice Blackmun noted in his dissent, the transfer of jurisdiction over crimes of sodomy stemmed less from an emergent interest by the king in prohibiting sodomy than it did from the obliteration of the Catholic Church's courts in England after the Crown's split with Rome. The catalog of previously purely ecclesiastical offenses was dumped in the laps of the secular judges.[14]

Chief Justice Burger wasn't content to stop there; he went on to quote a most onerous statement by William Blackstone, who in this lawyer's opinion can be blamed for much of what is wrong with the Anglo-

American legal system: "[T]he infamous crime against nature" is an offense of "deeper malignity" than rape; it is a heinous act "the very mention of which is a disgrace to human nature" and "a crime not fit to be named." In this bastion of separation of church and state, only Justice Blackmun, joined in dissent by Justices Brennan, Marshall, and Stevens, took issue with the religious underpinning of Georgia's condemnation of homosexual sex. "The core of [Georgia's] defense . . . ." Justice Blackmun wrote, "however, is that [Hardwick] and others who engage in conduct prohibited . . . interfere with Georgia's exercise of the 'right of the Nation and of the States to maintain a decent society.'" Blackmun continued, "Essentially, [Georgia argues], 'for hundreds of years, if not thousands, [homosexual acts] have been uniformly condemned as immoral' is a sufficient reason to permit a State to ban them today." Blackmun went on to admonish the assertion that:

> 'traditional Judeo-Christian values proscribe' the conduct involved cannot provide an adequate justification for [the Georgia law]. That certain, but by no means all, religious groups condemn the behavior at issue gives the State no license to impose their judgments on the entire citizenry. The legitimacy of secular legislation depends instead on whether the State can advance some justification for its law beyond its conformity to religious doctrine. Thus, far from buttressing [its] case, [Georgia's] invocation of Leviticus, Romans, St. Thomas Aquinas, and sodomy's heretical status during the Middle Ages undermines his suggestion that [the law] represents a legitimate use of secular coercive power. A state can no more punish private behavior because of religious intolerance than it can punish such behavior because of racial animus.[15]

It is shocking that the patently intolerant religious origins of Georgia's discrimination against gays did not persuade the nation's highest court that the law was inimical to our democratic values. Rather, the Court reinforced the fundamentalist position by framing the question not in terms of a right to sexual autonomy or to privacy in general, as Georgia's law on its face applied to both heterosexuals and homosexuals, but rather as whether the Constitution conferred a specific right to "engage in homosexual sodomy." In the last paragraph of his dissenting opinion, which reads like a collective sigh of America's gay citizens, Blackmun posits that:

[i]t took but three years for the Court to see the error in its analysis in *Minersville School District v. Gobitis* [a case requiring salute to the American flag over religious objection] and to recognize that the threat to national cohesion posed by a refusal to salute the flag was vastly outweighed by the threat to those same values posed by compelling such a salute. I can only hope that here, too, the Court soon will reconsider its analysis and conclude that depriving individuals of the right to choose for themselves how to conduct their intimate relationships poses a far greater threat to the values most deeply rooted in our Nation's history than tolerance of nonconformity could ever do. Because I think the Court today betrays those values, I dissent.[16]

Despite Blackmun's mustered hopefulness, it would be seventeen long years before gays had their vindication under the law.

The idea behind *Bowers v. Hardwick*, that Americans traditionally have been God-fearing people opposed to the abominations of homosexuality or any other deviation from their moral order and, consequently, that their laws were enacted to preserve righteousness, is the same distortion of America's founding ideals that is being perpetrated by Dobson, Falwell, Robertson, and their cohorts to millions of Americans every day. It is no wonder that such thinking found its way into the Supreme Court.

Exit polling showed that, more than defense or the economy, morality was the decisive factor for many citizens casting their votes in the 2004 election, helping George W. Bush to carry the Electoral College and be reelected president.[17] This concept of morality is, of course, amorphous. Morality can mean inclusiveness, respect for human dignity, or love of one's neighbor; it can mean what Dr. Martin Luther King Jr., referred to as *agape* love—in that sense morality is a mirror of the selfless, encompassing, and nonjudgmental love exemplified by Jesus of Nazareth in the New Testament. The gay person reading those exit polls, however, knows that the morality that carried away the voting public in no sense resembles the *agape* love preached by Jesus or King. The morality that helped to reelect George W. Bush is essentially Calvinistic in origin and philosophy. Consequently, this morality tells its adherents that man is inherently bad and can be forgiven and saved from his sin only by being born again. Some actions, choices, and lifestyles, including homosexuality, are undeniably sinful. They are to be warred against as the potential undoing of the Christian civilization established in the United States because they destroy the order created by those eminently Christian, doubtlessly born-again Founders who saw fit to create America. Sociologist Christian Smith found that evangelical Christians are most likely to adhere to a Calvinistic moral view, and, indeed, evangelicals were so important to Karl Rove's orchestration of Bush's reelection that Bush fervently came to support a federal constitutional amendment to ban gay marriage, an idea toward which he initially had remained cool.

Thus, when gays read the exit polling on morality, they see it as a dangerous signal of their continued oppression. Philosopher Alasdair MacIntyre bemoans the American desire to pursue "virtue." MacIntyre believes that moral judgments are never anything more than "expressions of preference, expressions of attitude or feeling." MacIntyre thus concludes that debates about abortion, gay rights, and other public arguments about morality are ultimately only divisive and "interminable."[18] But the rational answer to the dilemma MacIntyre posits is the assertion of the real Enlightenment-influenced American morality which, despite the contentions of Dobson et al. to the contrary, the Founders really intended. This is a public morality in which there is room for the competing views of the American polity and a morality in which none of these conflicting views is allowed to dominate or to be legislated but in which each view is paid an essential civic respect. The Founders believed in the morality of liberal democracy in which no one view of the right or proper way to live is allowed to drive out all others. This true American morality, however, as evidenced by the 2004 election, has been largely replaced (or, at least, displaced) by a fiction that tells Americans that the fundamentalist Christian morality of the Dobsons, the Robertsons, and the Falwells was the prevailing morality of the Founding era.

But the Dobsons, the Falwells, and the Robertsons are either pernicious in their untruths or they are the poorest students of American history one could fear to encounter. In fact, their only comment about the founding of our nation with which I would agree is a 1996 declaration by Robertson. "Jefferson," he said, "was much more of a Christian than many that claim to be Christian today."[19] With that I will wholeheartedly agree. At least Jefferson did not actively twist and distort the religion of Jesus into a religion of legalism and anger. Jefferson placed almost no credence in any single theology; instead, he concentrated on Jesus' gospel message of love. In fact, he was attacked by the self-righteous of his day as an atheist. But like the bigots of our day, his attackers mistook his nonconformity to their truth as antireligious sentiment, rather than recognizing his deep religious contemplation as valuable.

While still president, Jefferson began constructing what he believed to be the true Gospel. He cut and pasted portions of the Gospels into a notebook, removing those passages he believed to be contaminated by the zealous gloss of the centuries. In a letter to John Adams he wrote:

> To the Corruptions of Christianity, I am, indeed, opposed; but not to the genuine precepts of Jesus himself. I am a Christian in the only sense in which he wanted anyone to be: sincerely attached to his doctrines, in preference to all others; ascribing to himself every human excellence; and believing he never claimed any other.[20]

This acerbic comment to Adams indicates that Jefferson did not even accept the doctrine of Jesus' divinity. Jefferson had further disgust for the "tricks" (his word, not mine) played on Jesus' doctrines by zealots and fundamentalists. He despised a bedrock doctrine of today's fundamentalists— that all men are sinners, fallen from grace—and he abhorred any notion of an "elect." Jefferson is not alone. When John Adams became president, he actually signed a treaty that pointedly declared that "the government of the United States is not in any sense founded on the Christian religion." The Falwells, the Robertsons, and the Dobsons would have utterly disgusted the Jeffersons, the Adamses, and the Franklins. These men hated ignorance and superstition and they hated theocratic rule. After all, the framers had inherited an English history rife with church-state struggle and they learned important lessons from the havoc such entanglement wreaked on their not-so-distant motherland.

Moreover, Jefferson detested fundamentalism's aversion to knowledge and reason. He did not believe in divine revelation, the Trinity, the virgin birth of a divine god-child, or most other orthodox Christian doctrines. In a letter to a teenage nephew, Jefferson admonishes him to "[q]uestion with boldness even the existence of God; because, if there be one, he must more approve of the homage of reason, than that of blindfolded fear." He detested literalism, writing in the same letter: "[F]or example, in the book of Joshua, we are told, the sun stood still several hours." He then mocked the idea of inspiration behind such scripture. "But it is said that the writer of that book was inspired. Examine, therefore, candidly, what evidence there is of his having been inspired. The pretension is entitled to your inquiry, because millions believe it. On the other hand, you are astronomer enough to know how contrary it is to the law of nature that a body revolving on its axis, as the earth does, should have stopped, should not, by that sudden stoppage, have prostrated animals, trees, buildings, and should after a certain time have resumed its revolution, and that without a second general prostration." "Your reason," he wrote, "is the only oracle given you by Heaven, and you are answerable, not for the rightness, but the uprightness of the decision." These comments hardly betray a man taken with a Dobsonian view of religion.[21]

Thomas Paine, an instigator of American independence, wrote in his famous book, *The Age of Reason:* "This story [of the virgin birth of Christ] is upon the face of it, the same kind of story of Jupiter and Leda and Jupiter and Europa or any of the amorous adventures of Jupiter; and shows . . . that the Christian faith is built upon heathen mythology." Jefferson also wrote, "[T]he day will come when the mystical generation of Jesus by the Supreme Being as His Father, in the womb of a virgin, will be classed with the fable of the generation of Minerva in the brain of Jupiter."[22]

As for the Ten Commandments, often used to relegate homosexual love to sinful deviance, the Founders had equal disdain. Thomas Jefferson wrote to John Adams in 1824:

> Where did we get the ten commandments? [The Bible] itself tells us they were written by the finger of God on tables of stone, which were destroyed by Moses; it specified those on the second set of tables in different form and substance, but still without saying how the others were recovered. But the whole history of these books is so defective and doubtful, that it seems vain to attempt minute inquiry into it; and such tricks have been played with their text, and with the other texts of other books relating to them, that we have a right from the cause to entertain much doubt what parts of them are genuine.[23]

Paine shared similar reservations. There is "no internal evidence of divinity within them," he wrote. As for the Epistles of St. Paul, which frequently are recited to damn homosexuals, Jefferson considered Paul the "first corrupter of the doctrines of Jesus."[24]

Jefferson's rejection of orthodox Christian doctrine was not lost on his political enemies. Just as Robertson, today, would waste no time in attacking anyone who doesn't toe the religious right's line, Jefferson's political opponents branded him an infidel. They wrote gleefully of the two atheist "Toms" (Jefferson and Paine).

What would Jefferson think of today's religious right? I think he would have despised it. For instance, I recently saw Dobson on *Larry King Live*. He spent the hour deriding homosexuals and explaining why gay marriage would equal the destruction of the family—all, he claimed, supported by the Holy Scriptures. A caller asked Dobson an unrelated theological question, to which Dobson, apparently stumped, replied, "[W]ell, I'm no theologian." Here is a man presuming to educate King's viewers on the sinful nature of homosexuality, yet he is not a theologian! Jefferson, I think, would have been both amused at the enormous pomposity of Dobson's performance and saddened and disgusted that so many Americans buy Dobson's wares of ignorance—and, worse still, that they cast their ballots accordingly.

Fundamentalists' unabashed proclivity for hate speech and their willingness to distort history, not to mention the Gospel of Christ, for their own ends, explains why gay women and men have a suspicious aversion to fundamentalist religion in America. In fact, given the fundamentalists' success in branding themselves "Christian" and everyone else "non-Christian," I don't think it is an unfair response for gay men and women to be suspicious of *all* religion. When gays hear in the media that certain groups called "Christian" are working to block legal measures that would guarantee basic civil rights to gay people, they place that information within a centuries-old historical framework of persecution in the name of God.

Is this an overreaction on my part? Michael Perry, one of the defining voices in the academic analysis of the proper place of religious morality in law and politics and author of numerous books on the subject, including *Under God? Religious Faith in Liberal Democracy*, was kind enough to read a draft of this chapter. In correspondence, he raises the criticism that I overstepped in intimating "the demise of liberal democracy" by exaggerating the influence of the religious right. As my mentor and former teacher, Perry was the first person to stimulate me to think critically about the nexus of religion and American political life. But here Perry and I disagree. The 2004 election results are, I believe, bold indicators of just the kind of demise I see, but Perry doesn't see. If people exiting the November polls had said that they voted for George Bush because they felt safer because of his stance on terrorism, for example, I might have disagreed but I would not have been nearly as alarmed as I am now, knowing that exit polls showed a fundamentalist moral view as the predominant reason explaining votes cast to re-elect Bush—not to mention antigay amendments to the constitutions of eleven more states. Emboldened evangelicals, supported by traditionalist Catholics, have renewed their demands for a federal marriage amendment, challenged the teaching of evolution in favor of creationism in Georgia's public schools, and demanded that textbooks adopted by Texas schools be altered to reinforce the man-woman marriage definition. These things, I predict, are indicators of a disturbing turn to the right in America.

Our liberal democracy was founded on the ideals of the Enlightenment: a respect for science and rationality, a rejection of government by religion or superstition, and tolerance of competing views. In a postelection op-ed for the *New York Times,* poignantly titled "The Day the Enlightenment Went Out," historian Garry Wills noted that America is beginning to resemble less the secular nations of Western Europe and more the theocratic Muslim nations against which it is in seeming constant struggle.[25] In this great country, the first Enlightenment democracy, more people now believe in the virgin birth than in evolution, and, despite hard-learned lessons about equality and a Supreme Court decree about the inappropriateness of creationism for public education, these issues continue to emerge as fundamentalists tighten their grip on the presidency and the Congress and clamor for judicial and other appointments that will further their agenda. I, therefore, find that I must reluctantly join Wills in wondering whether the Enlightenment really has "gone out" of America.

But what exactly is the nature of the antigay fundamentalist argument? I seriously doubt that many fundamentalists themselves have put much thought into that question. For them, the basis of the argument is superfluous; the goal is to abide by an argument they neither think about nor understand but merely defend. To the extent that any real content to the argument can be discerned, however, the argument is bilinear. One line is the idea that the Bible is a direct revelation of God, a continuation of the idea that the Ten Commandments were written by the finger of God. The other is a more deist assertion that disapprobation for homosexuality is manifested in God's nature, that is, homosexuality is not natural. But inasmuch as the argument is bilinear, it is also unilinear, for each branch of the argument—direct revelation and unnaturalness—is traced to biblical interpretation.

Because of this commonality, I will attempt to address both arguments in the same discussion in this chapter. I address the fundamentalist religious argument, not because I really believe the argument should have any real influence on the way gays are treated in society, but because I believe that to give religion a determinative value in a discussion of homosexuality as a biological manifestation is to put on religion and on the Bible a weight they were not intended to bear—the weight of science. The scriptures, I believe, were not meant to be treated as scientific texts. I address the argument simply because it is, in the United States, such an important factor in the debate over homosexuality. Fundamentalist religious conviction, whether one likes it or not, has entered the moral and political debate over homosexuality currently taking place in the United States, and its arguments must be reckoned with. In that reckoning, it is important first to realize that the Bible has very little to say about homosexuality, period. In the original languages of the Old and New Testaments, the term *homosexual,* or its equivalent, is never used. It is also important to recognize that at every point in which same-sex sex acts are discussed, they occur within a wholly negative context—a context apart from the actual sexual acts themselves. Today, many serious biblical scholars—John Boswell in his book *Christianity, Social Tolerance, and Homosexuality*—for example, assert that homosexuality and Christianity are not incompatible.

The paramount story used to condemn homosexuality is the biblical story of Sodom and Gomorrah—from which the term *sodomite* is derived. The Sodom story (Genesis 19) has been widely interpreted as God's loathing of homosexual acts. The story is basically this: Angels in the form of men are sent to the city of Sodom and received at the home of Lot, a prominent resident. Lot's neighbors do not echo his hospitality toward the visitors. All the men of Sodom surround Lot's home, unaware that the strangers are in fact angels, and demand to "know" the visitors. They try physically to invade Lot's residence in order to "know" the visitors—a plan thwarted only when the angels miraculously strike the men of Sodom blind. Lot and his family are warned to flee Sodom, and, as punishment for their abominations, the city (along with its sister city, Gomorrah) and citizens are destroyed in a hail of fire and brimstone.

This story has been widely hailed as the epitome of God's judgment of homosexuals and the fate which he has assigned them. But this view is not universally believed; indeed, it is questioned by most serious students of the Bible. The story of Sodom is an ambiguity. Many scholars have pointed out that the Hebrew word translated as "know" in the Sodom story may mean just that—to see and be made aware of the character and intentions of the visiting angels. Genesis 19:9 indicates that Lot apparently had failed to acquire the requisite permission from the town elders to entertain the visitors in Sodom. Befitting the ambiguity of the Sodom story, laws against sodomy based upon interpretation of the tale often are unbelievably vague. Under the American system of federalism, depending upon jurisdiction, an anti-sodomy statute can preclude anal intercourse, only oral sex, or a combination of anal and oral intercourse by a combination of people—by all people, of whatever gender; by men only; or by homosexual actors only. But most commonly, such laws, even those neutral on their faces—that is, applicable regardless of sexual orientation—are targeted only at same-sex, usually male-on-male, sex.

What exactly is the nature of the Sodom story? As I see it, the story of Sodom and God's condemnation of Sodom is about an overall hostile and violent environment. For example, the idea perpetuated by some televangelists and fundamentalist preachers that Sodom was some sort of gay ghetto or commune is untenable: Its residents could not have been exclusively homosexual, for obvious reasons of procreation; Sodom was apparently a thriving center. *If*, and that is a big if, there was a sexual connotation to the Sodomites' assault on Lot's guests, it must have been a desire to degrade or punish them in some way—to treat them in the same way that women were treated (and in many instances continue to be treated) in the Middle East.

To treat a man like a woman is still a method of degradation today. For instance, delinquent youth may be threatened with the prospect of prison, where the convicts will "make a woman" out of them. Or, as another example, North Carolina Sheriff Gerald Hege (who incidentally had a highly rated program on Court TV before his entanglement in accusations of misappropriation of county resources) forced prisoners to wear pink prison jumpsuits—the association of pink with femininity was to degrade them. The "just" authors of the Bible apparently did not believe God's favor rested equally on women and men. For example, Lot offered his two virgin daughters to the crowd of assailants. Surely this is not an impulse with which the modern reader can identify. When the writer of the second Epistle of Peter in the New Testament describes Lot as "a good man" mortified by the godless, violent behavior of his neighbors, he has apparently forgotten this less-than-admirable side of a man who would sacrifice his own flesh and blood in such a horrific way. I suspect, as do many biblical scholars, that the attack on Lot's guests was motivated more by a desire to degrade and humiliate the august visitors than by any real sexual desire. The hysteric assertion by some fundamentalists that the actions of the men of Sodom were somehow *worse* because they would rather rape men than women should be seen as the irrational, baseless argument that it is. As the authors of *Is the Homosexual My Neighbor* rightly stress: "[E]ven if the angels had taken on the form of women for their earthly visitation, the desire of the men of Sodom to rape them would have been every bit as evil in the sight of God. And the rain of fire and brimstone would have been every bit as sure."[26]

Homosexuality is also condemned in Leviticus 18:22 and 20:13. However, John Boswell and others have noted that the mention of homosexuality in Leviticus comes in the so-called Holiness Code, which is concerned with ceremonial purity rather than with the intrinsic decency or indecency of any given act. This same grouping of scriptures condemns the wearing of garments made with different types of thread, the sowing of more than one type of seed in the same field, and sexual intercourse with a woman during her menstruation. Today no one would seriously assert the inherent evil of any of these things. Homosexuality is simply one item in a list of prohibitions that should not be read out of its ancient Hebrew context.

Moreover, with all spiritual deference, let us not give the obscurer passages of the Bible more credibility than they deserve. The Old Testament, particularly those passages dealing with Levirate life, is bursting with edicts that can be seen only as absurd by the modern reader. For example, Deuteronomy 22:28, 29 proclaims that an unwed woman raped by a man is to be bought by that man from her father and that she must remain married to her rapist all her life. Presumably, the impossibility of divorcing the woman is a punishment for the man's sin. Nothing at all is said of the woman's plight in this patriarchy. Mustn't that be hard to swallow for the modern Christian? Furthermore, one must consider Deuteronomy 23:2, which directs that "[n]o one whose testicles have been crushed or whose penis has been cut off may be admitted into the community of the Lord"; the admonition to stone the community's unchaste women in Deuteronomy 22:21; and the peculiar passage of Deuteronomy 25:11–12 that states, "When two men are fighting and the wife of one intervenes to save her husband from the blows of his opponent, if she stretches out her hand and seizes the latter by his private parts, you shall chop off her hand without pity." The litany could continue, but surely this is evidence that the prohibition against homosexual conduct is but one in a list of restrictions that have no legitimacy outside the confines of the ancient, war-making society by which they were conceived—if, indeed, they had any legitimacy at the time of their conception.

Furthermore, for a group of Christians bent on the divergence of Christ's teachings from those of Judaism, Jesus' own commentary and that of the New Testament appear to carry little weight with them. In the Gospel of Luke, for example, Jesus refers to the destruction of Sodom in the context of inhospitality, not of homosexuality—a particularly peculiar analogy for Christ to make if his Father indeed destroyed Sodom out of abhorrence of homosexual sex acts. In other places in the New Testament, though not by Jesus himself, the destruction of Sodom is linked to sex. The Book of Jude, for example, indicates that Sodom was destroyed because of "sexual immorality" and "unnatural lust." But isn't it just as likely that the "sexual immorality" and "unnatural lust" spoken of is a reference to the attempt of the Sodomites to gang rape the angels? If the Sodom story is condemning homosexuality—why doesn't someone say so?

Reference to homosexual acts per se is made only once in the New Testament, by Saint Paul in the first chapter of his Epistle to the Romans. Again, it is not necessary to accept the notion that the remonstrance in Romans is an attack on homosexuality for homosexuality's sake. The larger context of this portion of Romans is a denouncement of idolatry and a general falling away from God. As Paul's mission and writing were undeniably influenced by the Greek culture in which he lived, it is likely that Paul was denouncing the connection of homosexuality with male temple prostitution, which constituted an integral part of some Greco-Roman religious practices. If this passage is, as I and many others view it, directed at the backslider and the denier of God, how then is it applicable to the sincere homosexual Christian? How is it applicable to the monogamous, genuinely loving homosexual partnership? For as much as Paul decries lust, he has no comparable decrial of genuine love. As Pope John Paul II has said, "Every genuinely human love is a reflection of the love that is God himself."[27] To then say that some kinds of love are qualitatively better than others and to condemn God's creation on the basis of it must surely be a brutish evil.

Furthermore, Paul was a Jew. As such, his distaste for many elements of the gentile world that were anathema to Jewish legalism is apparent in his writing; often what he spoke of as "nature" isn't really natural at all, but rather a reflection of accepted Jewish social customs. For example, Paul writes in I Corinthians of the natural degradation inherent in a man having long hair or, by negative implication, a woman having short hair. It should be quite obvious to anyone with a cursory knowledge of biology that the hair of both men and women will grow long if left to nature's design. Whether, or how, men and women cut their hair is purely a social construct. Thus, Paul's intimation that homosexual acts are unnatural could easily be viewed as his acknowledgment that they were contrary to the traditional Jewish social model rather than an indication that they are, in fact, contrary to God's natural design.

Finally, even if I were to concede the Bible's condemnation of unnatural homosexuality, it is important to note that the Bible includes no discourse on the state of nature that is homosexuality. All arguable instances of disapprobation for homosexuality in the biblical context are aimed at an unnatural indulgence in homosexual sex acts by people who are evidently not of the homosexual orientation. The homosexual practices we encounter in the Bible are always inextricably linked to the arbitrary exertion of power to dominate through rape, adultery, and so on. The sexual activity targeted is always a manifestation of dominance and abuse. Nowhere is the genuine romantic love of one man for another or of one woman for another degraded or derided. For that reason, Paul's apparent disapproval of homosexuality could be viewed as disapproval of an inherently abusive social structure, not of homosexual orientation itself. I think of it in terms of Paul's treatment of slavery in Philemon. Slaveholders in the antebellum South used what they termed Paul's "approval" of the institution of slavery by his sending Onesimus back to his master. But a more accurate reading of Philemon, while it indeed shows Paul observing Roman law and returning a fugitive slave to his owner, also shows Paul taking the opportunity to critique the institution of slavery and to admonish Onesimus's master to embrace Onesimus upon his return—not as a slave but as a fellow human being.

FUNDAMENTALISM AND
THE ECSTASY OF TRUTH . . .

I believe there is much support for the idea that homophobia is a product of the inquisitional Catholic hysteria of an age far removed from the world of the Bible's authors, which was then seized upon by fundamentalist Protestant groups who appear to be sex-obsessed regardless of who is having the sex. In summing up my examination of the biblical foundation of fundamentalist homophobia, it is imperative to say that I do not believe for an instant that Paul or any other of the writers of the Old or New Testaments understood homosexuality as a natural, lifelong orientation. Understanding homosexuality in those terms is a relatively recent sociological advancement. I point out the different interpretive arguments simply to say that there is no way we can rationally and concretely decipher a biblical understanding of homosexuality. As I said at the beginning of this discussion, the Bible was not intended—surely we must see that—to be a scientific text explaining biology. It simply cannot bear that weight with integrity. Of course, religion has had little problem condemning people on the basis of biology. For instance, Deuteronomy 23:3 says, "No mamzer shall enter the assembly of YHVH, even to the tenth generation." "Mamzer" is usually translated "bastard." Obviously we can't choose our parents; some of us get adulterers or fornicators and some of us get much, much worse. Responsible believers should see that the Bible lacks any discernible truth by which we can understand homosexual orientation; therefore, we must look to science, and, perhaps more logically, to homosexuals themselves in order to understand homosexuality. The Christian fundamentalist's refusal to do so and his continual use of the Bible to justify hatred and inequality are grotesque distortions of the Bible's, or at least the Gospel's, overarching messages of love and inclusiveness.

Legalistic fundamentalist Christianity, with its focus on the ugliest possible interpretations of the Bible, has a pronounced following in the United States. Take, for example, the fundamentalist men's group, Promise Keepers. The group was originally founded in 1990 by Bill McCartney, former head football coach at the University of Colorado and, incidentally, an outspoken supporter of Colorado's Amendment 2. The organization grew from a small local movement to a thriving national organization with hundreds of thousands of men attending its meetings and rallies. In the mid-nineties, a very close friend of mine became involved with the organization and attended its rallies. I asked him what they talked about, what they hoped to accomplish. The goal, I discovered, was to reconstitute the modern family into some fifties-esque image of what the ideal family should be. The first thing glaringly apparent is the Promise Keepers' focus on the Pauline doctrine that wives must submit themselves to their husbands. Indeed, in order to keep the organization free from woman's weakening influence, women are strongly discouraged from attending Promise Keepers meetings. The organization toes the fundamentalist line that God ordained the husband to be the boss. Indeed, the Promise Keepers are fixated on traditional gender roles (you'll find Dobson's gender-obsessive essays among their official texts).

Less readily apparent than the group's determination to return women to subjection is its distrust and fear of homosexuals. In keeping with the disturbing reemergence of such psychological quackery, the Promise Keepers have allowed reformed ex-gay ministers to speak at their rallies, peddling the message that salvation will equal deliverance from homosexuality. Like Dobson's Focus on the Family organization, with which it is closely allied, Promise Keepers seems to long wistfully for a day when 1950s values and social structures were the norm (although Promise Keepers stresses the importance of racial equality). Principally, the distinction between male and female—with the traditional male role being dominant—is central to their particular brand of theology. It is no wonder, then, that the group's primary constituency is the white, middle-aged, middle-class, fundamentalist Protestant. It is precisely this group that feels most threatened by any societal impulse toward inclusiveness. Promise Keepers and Focus on the Family, in their encouragement of male dominance at the expense of women's and gay rights, conveniently overlook one thing. Saint Paul, whatever else he may have said, wrote in Galatians 3:28 that in Christ "there is no such thing as . . . male and female." In any case, to the proposition that there is a superior, dominant social position inherent in the heterosexual male, I can do little better than to quote nineteenth-century woman's rights advocate Sarah Grimké.

> Even admitting that Eve was the greater sinner, it seems to me that man might be satisfied with the dominion he has claimed and exercised for nearly 6000 years, and that more true nobility would be manifested by endeavoring to raise the fallen and invigorate the weak than by keeping women [and gays] in subjection.[28]

Pat Robertson, with his constant fixation on God's anger and wrath against almost everyone who doesn't fit his restrictive vision of the Christian, is, I believe, less dangerous to the gay individual in America than groups like Promise Keepers and Focus on the Family. Unlike Robertson, they cloak their hatefulness in feigned compassion. At the helm of Focus on the Family, for example, is James Dobson, who is masterful at painting a portrait of American life—if America were to embrace his particular fundamentalism—that would move Norman Rockwell to inspiration. His radio program and his writings are full of wholesome stories about his idyllic life in the 1950s and about how much better off—how genuinely better off— we would be if we were to return to this type of world order: the stay-at- home mom, the unquestioned father/boss, the obedient, contented children—and the homosexual, of course, locked quietly in the closet. Or, I suppose, better still, married with children in postwar suburbia. Focus on the Family literature concentrates on loving the homosexual but hating his sin. The literature is full of testimonials by so-called reformed gay men who have been delivered from homosexual demons by the love of Christ. The family, Dobson posits, will be safe only when homosexuality is eradicated. The homosexual is the perfect scapegoat for the perceived evils of a hu- manistic society, for they are, in the view of most fundamentalists, their exact opposite and, therefore, undeniably evil. Ah, the good old days— Dobson's rhetoric is one great sigh for a lustrous yesteryear. The negative side of the 1950s is, of course, never rehearsed. But as Bruce Bawer has put it, "[Dobson's voice] is the voice of every middle-class white heterosexual male who feels that everything was just fine in the old days, when blacks didn't dare cry out against their oppression, gays huddled voicelessly in the closet, and women were meek, pliant housewives."[29] Amen, I say. Amen.

We must remember, however, Saint Paul's admonition in Galatians 3:27–28:

Baptized into Christ,
you are clothed in Christ,
so that there is no more
Jew or Greek,
slave or free,
man or woman,
but all are one, are the same
in Christ Jesus.

It follows by implication that there is neither heterosexual nor homo- sexual, for this statement holds all the wisdom and all the truth of the Gospel message—in Christ's eyes we are all human beings of equal worth and dignity, equally deserving of God's love and of the love of one another. Herein lies the ultimate controversy between legalistic fundamentalist Christians and the rest of society. It is a clash of perspectives in which there is room for only one reality. The Episcopal Church in the United States faced a dilemma when the parishioners of New Hampshire elected an openly gay priest as their bishop. The rumble that followed in the Episcopal Church (although one doesn't automatically think of it as fundamentalist) provides a perfect picture of the dichotomy we face today. On one side of the debate were the reactionary legalists who predicted the end of the church if the election of a gay bishop were to be confirmed by the greater church. The deviance perspective called for the repression of the move to homosexual inclusion, while the diversity perspective fought to fit the question into a framework of responsibility and rationality—they were concerned more with *what kind* of bishop a particular gay priest would make, rather than with *what* homosexuals were or were not in general.

The same dichotomous clash is played out in many churches: The Catholic Church issued a statement in 1992 calling homosexuality an "objective disorder" (long after psychologists had ceased to see it as a disorder). That statement, unfortunately, pales in comparison to the Vatican's statements in the wake of the *Lawrence v. Texas* decision, in which the Vatican equates homosexuals with child abusers and calls the world's legislators to unite in a campaign against the advancement of gay rights. In 1993, the Southern Baptist Convention voted to expel from membership any congregations that "act to affirm, approve, or endorse homosexual behavior."[30] Its antagonism toward gays was so strong that the Southern Baptist Convention was willing to compromise its enduring devotion to the autonomy of the local congregation in order to stamp out those churches that might reach out to homosexuals not as deviant sinners in need of redemption but as loving and love-worthy members of the body of Christ. In the ten years that have passed since that move, the position of the Southern Baptist Convention has not softened. Recently in my community a Baptist church was expelled from the state Baptist convention for refusing to repudiate homosexuality (the church had baptized homosexuals).

There are, of course, principled voices in this wilderness of homophobia. San Francisco's Dolores Street Baptist Church, for example, voted to withdraw from the Southern Baptist Convention even before an expulsion measure passed. Dolores Street Baptist issued a statement saying: "We cannot support and stand with a denomination that as a matter of policy condemns and excludes a part of our family: lesbian, gay, and bisexual women and men."[31] The Dolores Street congregation personifies the benefits of lighting a candle rather than cursing the darkness. They reached out to the gay community and proved that, even in the bowels of fundamentalism, there is, indeed, redemption to be found.

CONCLUSIONS: SOCIAL AND RELIGIOUS . . .

So what does fundamentalism mean for the generations of lesbians and gay men coming of age in the twenty-first century? It inevitably means they will face some homophobia. No single issue gives occasion for more un-Christian hatefulness in the name of Christianity than the issue of homosexuality. Thus far I have canvassed the evolution of gay rights through American history, culminating in the decade of the 1990s. Pitifully, many of the unpleasant events of that decade would not be out of place in the first decade of the twenty-first century. In 1992, the Southern Baptist Convention voted overwhelmingly to oust two North Carolina churches, one in Raleigh and the other in Chapel Hill, for endorsing homosexuality by blessing a homosexual union and licensing a gay man to preach. More than a decade later, on October 6, 2003, the Associated Press reported that the Baptist State Convention of North Carolina voted to expel another North Carolina church for accepting two gay men as members and baptizing them. In July 1992, the Vatican issued a directive urging Roman Catholic bishops in the United States to oppose laws that promoted public acceptance of homosexual conduct. In July 2003, the Vatican issued a twelve-page document addressed to the world's legislators: "To vote in favor of a law [a law that would recognize gay marriage or allow gays to adopt children] so harmful to the common good is gravely immoral."[32]

Still, I am hopeful. The age-old belief that there is only one position a Christian can take regarding homosexuality—that it is sinful—is eroding. As often as the old battles are being fought, a few are put to rest, and in an increasing number of instances homophobia has seen its last fight; and it is not victorious. Take, for example, the 1996 trial of the Episcopal bishop Walter Righter. Righter was tried for violating canon law by ordaining an openly gay man as a priest. In 2003, the Episcopal Church in America confirmed its first openly gay bishop. Although the confirmation was not without controversy, the Episcopal Church got a gay bishop just the same; and homophobia, if not defeated, at least grimaced at the blow. More than a decade after its monstrous decision, based principally on fundamentalist religious argument, *Bowers v. Hardwick* is no longer the law of the land, and homophobia is left with visible wounds.

Of course, I have no illusions that good will completely triumph over homophobia in every sphere. As long as there is a marginalized segment of this society still claiming a foothold on the periphery by placing its foot squarely on the skull of the one group it can find that has borne more derision than it, and as long as there is still a mean-spirited Robertson, Falwell, or Dobson to speak for that group, homophobia will be with us. Fundamentalist, legalistic religion has been used to justify a host of historical ills in this country and others: slavery, the subjugation of women, the deprivation of life-saving medical treatment to children, and so on. Over time, however, fundamentalism's hold on these abhorrent institutions has loosened and the deprived have arisen from the legalist's vice. The truly moral consciousness of society has triumphed over hate and evil. I am hopeful that, if not within the legalistic traditions themselves, this will happen for homosexuals on the broader plain of general society. Vermont and Massachusetts have recognized gay couples; private and municipal employers are granting recognition and equal benefits to gay employees more frequently; and the most intimate relations of gay individuals can no longer be branded criminal. Despite the all-too-often dismal shadow cast by American religion on homosexuality in this country, America is not a theocracy, but a democracy in which the inclinations of the majority are not to ride roughshod over the rights of the minority. The efforts of fundamentalists—and even of some in mainline religious groups—to restrict the civic status and private happiness of homosexuals in this country are the anathema of the concept of the universal worth and human dignity common to mankind that Jefferson and the other Founders endorsed at the inception of our nation. The word "unpatriotic" has been severely overused since September 11, 2001, but no acts are more deserving of the term than the efforts of the religious right against homosexuals in this country. Such efforts are unpatriotic and un-American, and more and more they are being recognized as such.

A purely social, or political, or legal resolution of the problem of homophobia, however, is not a satisfactory answer because religion has had such a pronounced role in creating and giving longevity to the monster. I write as a Christian, and societal vindication cannot completely answer my concerns about the young men who serve as the genesis for my thoughts here. Programs of democratic politics are most often posed to specifically political questions; they do not and cannot bring moral answers to essentially religious dilemmas. What then is the answer for the gay man or woman who has been so bruised by legalistic religion that he or she has become disenchanted with faith altogether?

For century upon century, blood has been shed and persecutions perpetrated in the name of God. Given Christianity's sordid history, it is a wonder that anything of Christ can be found in our churches today. Yet, I believe, He is there; and that is hope. For that hope to be translated to the young men mentioned at the beginning of this chapter, several things must happen: The true churches of love in this country should confront homophobia directly; so far, many of them are doing a poor job of it. They must shout Christ's greatest commandment, "love one another," from the rooftops; they must demonstrate, by direct action, the love of God to the homosexual. If the fundamentalist fiercely clings to manipulated untruths about the unnaturalness of homosexuality at the expense of the commandment to love, the churches of love must proclaim the manifest truth of love with equal tenacity. Perhaps if this lesson of love is taught with conviction, homosexuals will learn that to be gay does not automatically equal being a secularist.

If the churches must embrace the great commission of announcing God's love with more conviction, gays must embrace an equally important truth: We *are* loved. We are loved despite what particular congregations have to say about us, and we have a right to disagree—to assert ourselves and our inherent equality as children of God and as members of the human family.

Being gay does not mean that one must bear the ennui of a faithless life. We deserve to celebrate our faith but we needn't be beaten down and subjugated by that faith, as was my friend from the Baptist church. I am a dissident Catholic, at least when it comes to the church's stance on many social issues; I find the message of Cardinal Ratzinger, head of the Catholic Church's Congregation on the Doctrine of Faith (sadly, now Pope Benedict XVI), in many instances deplorable. But I am a Catholic, and I assert my right to be a Catholic. I am asked by many people, "Why are you, or why do you remain, a Catholic?" The answer is simple: I am a convert to Catholicism because I believe in the creed, in the sacraments, and I am comforted by the communion of saints and by the church's apostolic foundation. That does not mean that I must agree with every wrongheaded pronouncement coming from Rome about birth control or the service of altar girls or other issues having no more relation to the love content that is Christ than the color of the carpeting in any given church. Historian and

author Garry Wills put it succinctly in his book, *Why I Am a Catholic*. Wills
wrote:

> Troubled belief is not disbelief, though "true believers" take it for that
> . . . An unexamined faith is not a faith. It is a superstition. The process
> of questioning one's faith is one that I have undergone with many, if
> not most, believers, most certainly with the ones who said they shared
> my critical attitude toward the people without losing their funda-
> mental commitment to the church.[33]

I couldn't agree more with those sentiments. For years as a Southern Baptist, I fretted about the incompatibility of my own ideas about salvation,
Christology, and, of course, homosexuality with the official position of the
church. As a Catholic, I have fretted primarily about the church's position
regarding homosexuality but also about its position on women clergy,
celibacy, and other matters. When I spoke out, I worried: "What if my priest
gives me the cold shoulder?" "What if I am shunned by my fellow parishioners?" I worried about what the friends of my Southern Baptist grandmother would think to hear me defending homosexuality and criticizing the
exclusivity of fundamentalist, legalistic traditions, like that of the Baptists.
But eventually came the moment when I just didn't care anymore, the moment I realized that I *am* a Christian, as much as anyone else, no matter
what they say about me. In *A Place at the Table*, Bruce Bawer reports a sermon by Bishop Edmond L. Browning of the Episcopal Church to a gay Epis-
copalian organization in which Browning posed the question this way:

> Is it possible to know the pain of what you have known and still feel it
> within yourself to remain in the body where so much of that pain has
> occurred? Can you be the reconcilers Christ calls all of us to be with-
> out either denying the reality of your pain on the one hand or denying
> the possibility of its coming to an end on the other, without either
> minimizing what you have felt or allowing it to overcome you?[34]

For me, the answer is YES. I don't need to leave the Catholic Church because I am homosexual and I don't need to acquiesce in anyone else's definition of Christian. How awesome it would be if every struggling gay
Christian, indeed gay person of any faith, could come to that conclusion.

Today, millions of legalistic Christians try to tell us that if we don't believe their interpretation of the Bible then we aren't Christian at all. They are consumed with what they say we *should* be. But, for me, the most powerful part of Jesus' ministry is his constant accent on presence. God is not in the *should be,* but in the *is.* If God is really the great I Am, then he is all of us. Saying to a gay person, "I love you, but I hate this core part of you," creates a constant atmosphere of public contempt and derision that is as equal to an attack on the soul as any human being can feel in this life. But if God is the I Am, if he is present in each of us, then it is equally an attack on Him.

The legalists have been morbidly obsessed with what happened when Moses came down from the mountain—the multiplication of laws and rituals—rather than being concerned with what happened on the mountain, which was God's presence in the imperfect human world. Ironically, they miss the event because their view is obscured by the scaffolding of rules and regulations they build in order to garner a better view. That has been the primary religious conflict of history. But the place of the gay individual in that conflict is hopeful. As a minister friend of mine said, "I know that the Lord will not abandon His church, but I hope He keeps reforming her over and over . . . 'til we are formed into the image of Christ." Until that time, we have only to embrace our faith as we know it and tangibly experience it. And sometimes, at bottom, that is to have faith in ourselves; because, in matters of faith, there is never a "that's that," nor will there ever be.

PART 2

Seekers after happiness, all who follow
The convolutions of your simple wish,
It is later than you think; nearer that day
Far other than that distant afternoon . . .

—W. H. Auden

CHAPTER 3

Gay Citizenship

The Politics of Transformation

A nation, as a society, forms a moral person, and every member of it is personally responsible for his society.

—Thomas Jefferson

Gays in America have fewer rights than do barnyard animals in Sweden.

—Richard Mohr

FROM THE FOUNDING YEARS of the republic right through the nineteenth century, most sex laws were passed with the intent of strengthening marriage. They were not necessarily passed—at least not overtly—with the intention of subjugating the homosexual. In fact, until the hysteria of McCarthyism, gays were just a blip on the American cultural radar; the homosexual was crowded to the fringes more than he was crushed directly. But heterosociety's reactionary response to the perceived homosexual threat to its hegemonic domination in the postwar years brought about a radical redefinition of the American citizen. If, in the era roughly defined as pre-Stonewall, the gay person suffered as much from invisibility as from outright homophobic aggression, the 1950s and 1960s saw a radical shift, a confining of what it meant to be American to a narrow, rigid concept: patriotic, hardworking, heterosexual, Christian, married, and childbearing.

(Or, in the feminine corollary, stay-at-home wife and mom). Heterosexuality swiftly turned into a condition of American citizenship and a prerequisite to the pursuit of happiness.

A poignant example is the ultraconservative reactions of the 1970s to the perceived liberalness of the 1960s. Through efforts led by evangelical singer Anita Bryant and the fundamentalist Save Our Children organization, for example, 1977 saw voters in Dade County, Florida, repeal a six-month-old ordinance prohibiting discrimination based on sexual orientation. Throughout the 1970s, a trend prevailed toward striking down equal rights ordinances. Gays were again on the run as police and other violence against them escalated to a fever pitch. A new kind of conservative right had crystallized in reaction to the inroads made by liberals in the 1960s and early 1970s. Gays weren't the only targets of this strident campaign; the equal rights amendment went down in a blaze, and the *Roe v. Wade* decision, securing the right of pregnant women to choose abortion, seemed in peril. While our Western European counterparts, like France and Germany, were making humanitarian progress, the United States seemed gripped in a vice of new, or newly empowered, conservatism.

The crushing blow came when San Francisco councilman Harvey Milk and reform-minded Mayor George Moscone were murdered by a former police officer and councilman Dan White, a gay rights opponent. Adding insult to injury was White's acquittal on the charges of murder, largely orchestrated by police witnesses testifying to White's paramount character (Gore Vidal has noted, characteristically, "It is no secret that American police rarely observe the laws of the land when out wilding with each other, and as any candid criminal judge will tell you, perjury is often their native tongue in court.") and psychiatric testimony of White's diminished capacity because of his junk food diet (the now infamous Twinkie defense).[1] The jury, from which gays had been excluded, convicted White of manslaughter, and he received a sentence of seven years and eight months—hardly the death sentence possible for the murder of public officials in California. On the day of the verdict, thousands marched on San Francisco's city hall in protest. The protests turned violent, resulting in property damage and the torching of several police cruisers; police retaliated by beating gays at various bars on Castro Street.

Yet amid these bleak times, something extraordinary happened. Gays under siege had formerly gone running for cover into the awaiting closet. But this time, they resisted. Gay liberationists did not disappear under the onslaught; they regrouped and reemerged, bent on advancing their cause or, at least, not losing the ground they had gained. They resisted. By fits and starts, gays got around to becoming not aliens, but citizens. This awakening, perhaps reawakening, of gay political attentiveness was again evident in 1991 when gays in California, furious at their betrayal by Republican Governor Pete Wilson's refusal to sign a bill (which he had promised to sign in his campaign bid for gay votes) that would have protected gays from discrimination in employment, took to the streets in mass demonstrations. In Los Angeles, these demonstrations occurred day after day for weeks, crippling traffic in sections of the city. "We're here. We're queer. Get used to it!" rang from street corners, while the demonstrations gained momentum daily. The emotional furor perpetuating these protests proved unsustainable, but they are exemplary of a certain attentiveness, a communal political cohesion largely unseen prior to the 1970s. This acceptance of responsibility was—and has been—key to the advances in gay rights decades later. Gays began to channel their private hurt into public action.

Part of becoming citizens and embracing citizenship for gays is accepting the reality that our private lives cannot remain private. Sometimes this realization brings discomfort and exposes the most vulnerable parts of ourselves to injury and insult. Yet, when the outside world persists in defining us by our sexual orientation and in basing the very nature of our citizenship on that intimate aspect of our lives, we cannot responsibly continue with a privacy-at-all-costs method of operation. I know countless gay people who say that their sexual orientation is a private matter and not one that they will allow to define their politics, their religion, their work. Yet this very thing that they wish to separate from the outside world is the thing that the world uses to define and, generally, to degrade them. By adopting such a posture, they are made complicit in the denial of their own dignity.

THE ABSENCE OF POLITICS . . .

The discussion of gay issues is often a discussion of binaries: gay/straight, natural/unnatural, majority/minority, knowledge/ignorance. As I have intimated, one of the most powerful and important binaries that must be discussed in ascertaining the place of the gay person in society is the public/private dichotomy. This is so because gay people often participate in a counterproductive dialogue, invariably discussing the content of their democratic citizenship in terms of their right to privacy. The right to pri-

vacy in consensual sexual relationships certainly is not a right I would disparage; it is, in my view, a human right, a constitutional right. But stopping
there indulges the fallacious presumption that being gay has only a sexual
component. As I have elucidated, it is much more. We should be able to be
gay as much publicly as privately. As Eve Sedgwick has noted, casting gay
rights in only the terms of a privacy question is a dangerous definition of political power as the right to keep one's sexuality in that special, unyielding
place where it belongs.

The danger is nowhere more evident than in the legal response to the
inequities faced by gays and lesbians in this country. *Bowers v. Hardwick,*
the case that made gays second-class citizens without the right to privacy in
their sexual relationships, and *Lawrence v. Texas,* the case vindicating a
right to privacy for gay individuals, were both about this public/private du-
ality. *Lawrence* undid the *Bowers* court's denial of privacy, but it did little to
assert a public right to be equal as homosexuals. In fact, the court carefully
enunciated that *Lawrence* was *not* about other more public rights—specifically marriage. Perhaps the danger is more apparent in the 1985 case of
Rowland v. Mad River Local School District in which an employee of the
school system was fired; ostensibly not because of her *private* sexual orientation (even the school system appeared to make a concession here), but
because of the employee's forthrightness with colleagues about her sexuality.[2]
The federal appellate court upheld the dismissal, holding that the employee
could be fired because the revelation of one's sexual orientation—coming
out—is not a matter of public concern and, therefore, is not protected
speech under the First Amendment. *Bowers* simply made it not private
either.

These cases illustrate that, as a minority striving for full equality, gays
cannot exist solely in the private realm. No matter how much we might like
to deny it, our biggest hurts are public hurts. The biggest inequitable hurdles that we must clear are those of the public realm. Inasmuch as people in
a democratic society can alter public life, they usually do so through public,
political institutions. Gays are guilty of a self-defeating neglect of the necessary public mechanisms of their political inhesion. Indeed, our neglect of
political institutions is the source of much of the instability and insecurity
in our private lives. The political and civic institutions that create, shape,
and enforce laws and define communities—and our active and conscientious involvement in them—are necessary because without them many of
the intensely private and personal aspects of our lives would not be possi-

ble. Often, threats to our personal privacy come from an inquisitorial and dictatorial public domain suspicious of those who are different from the homogeneous ideal. Thus, our neglect of our public responsibilities will not only perpetuate our public inequality but also will ultimately threaten the privacy we often prize above all else.

Gays cannot be blamed unsympathetically for this inattentiveness to things public. The closet has served well those who work to marginalize and disenfranchise gay Americans. Gays, particularly since the mid-twentieth century, have been beaten back and indoctrinated with the idea that they are weak, subordinate, and incapable of bettering themselves to any appreciable degree. We effectively have been told that the quality of our life is beyond our control, in the hands of a stronger ruling class that must be genuflected to in matters of equality and quality of life. Gays are taught a contempt for weakness and, thereby, a contempt for themselves. This contempt for the weak is part of the broader American social ecology in which we are taught to respect those who fight their way to the top, disregarding the welfare of any who stand in their way. Indeed, it is not even an American phenomenon; its most brutalizing manifestation must be Nazism.

In his book, *Our Contempt for Weakness*, Harald Ofstad writes:

If we examine ourselves in the mirror of Nazism we see our own traits—enlarged but so revealing for that very reason. Anti-Semitism is not the essence of Nazism. Its essence is the doctrine that the 'strong' shall rule over the 'weak,' and that the 'weak' are contemptible because they are 'weak.' Nazism did not originate in the Germany of the 1930s and did not disappear in 1945. It expresses deeply rooted tendencies, which are constantly alive in and around us. We admire those who fight their way to the top, and are contemptuous of the loser. We consider ourselves rid of Nazism because we abhor the gas chambers. We forget that they were the ultimate product of a philosophy which despised the 'weak' and admired the 'strong.'

The brutality of Nazism was not just the product of certain historical conditions in Germany. It was also the consequence of a certain philosophy of life, a given set of norms, values and perceptions of reality. We are not living in their situation but we practice many of the same norms and evaluations.[3]

Those who perpetrate sexual apartheid in this country are chief examples of the verity of Ofstad's evaluation. Even they, however, cannot bear the entire blame, swept up as they are in our society's tendency to form hierarchies of human worth in every conceivable aspect.

One of the true travesties of this way of life is the inevitable generation of self-hatred in the victim. The oppressed inevitably end up internalizing the value sets they see in the greater society; they begin to wonder if the definitions assigned to them are not apt descriptors of their being. Consequently, the engendered self-hate results in a shirking of the duties concomitant with responsible humanity. Self-worth and quality of life are left for others to decide, to define, to dictate. If, then, the oppressed person is dissatisfied, he can shrug his shoulders and blame the oppressors.

More frequently than not, the oppressed, at least subconsciously, blames himself as well. A massively negative self-image strips his ability to stand up for himself and to participate, even when possible, in the shaping of his own destiny. This sense of powerlessness translates to an often intense hatred of himself and those like him. Desmond Tutu has noted this "destructive internecine strife" within the African American community. Tutu writes: "You hate yourself and destroy yourself by proxy when you destroy those who are like this self you have been conditioned to hate."[4] With respect to gays, this is evidenced in American society by those men who, fearing their own subsurface desires and sexual awakenings, resort to gay bashing in order to smash to smithereens that part of themselves they have been taught to despise. Within the gay community itself, certain assimilationists blame prejudice and antigay feeling on those gays who are just "too queer" for their own good. All of this is part of the social ecology that has taught us to hate the weak and that, if we find ourselves in the ranks of the weak, we have no other recourse but to leave our fate to those strong ones destined to rule over us. For many gays in America, it means an absence of politics, an eclipse of attentiveness to the public world that defines us both publicly and privately.

A RETURN TO POLITICS . . .

And so to the Mattachine inquiries we might add a fourth, equally important and equally vital question: How shall we live? However we individually might choose to answer such an inquiry, it should be evident that there is little chance of achieving our elucidated goal but by practicing what I will call transformative politics. By definition, this politic aims at social change; as a breadth politic, it acknowledges and strives for arguments as inclusive as possible in their nature in order to persuade people to do the right thing, rather than focusing merely on rigid, often alienating, legalities. This is a politic of integration that insists on full equality for the small minority that is homosexual as a result of involuntary, immutable biology; and it insists on giving these people equality without asking any member of this biological group and legal category to sacrifice his personality, his individuality—his basic, inherent, irreducible human dignity. Transformative politics works for the end of public, government-sponsored discrimination aimed at this insular group and also calls for an end to government complicity in enforcing, actively or by omission of action, private discriminatory conduct with ultimately public consequences. These things it does with the knowledge that the law has an effect on the prevailing public culture which, in turn, influences further legal development: The cycle can be vicious, but it can also be redemptive. The focus of transformative politics is the implementation of public, political equality, not merely some formulary of civil tolerance. It is, I venture to say, the quickest route out of the mire that is now the politics of sexuality in the United States.

What does transformative politics mean in practice? William Eskridge has coined the terminology equality practice, and this is exactly what transformative politics is. It means, quite simply, equality: Gays would be able to join the armed services while affirming every aspect of their identity; government agencies and public corporations (at least those not so small or closely held that they could escape scrutiny for prejudicial hiring practices based on race or gender) could no longer discriminate with impunity; employment and housing discrimination would end; and equal opportunity would exist in marriage. Homosexuals would be elevated on constitutional par with at least the protections afforded against gender-based discrimination—a requirement that the actor show an important justification, more than a private animus against gay people, before being allowed to exclude any member of this group.

Some, perhaps many, heads have nodded until I reached the provision to end housing and employment discrimination. Yes, I mean exactly that transformative politics would work for antidiscrimination legislation applicable to private employers and proprietors who otherwise would treat an individual punitively based on that individual's sexual orientation. This is not, as some critics will assert, a departure from my statement that transformative politics is aimed at *public* reform. Public identities inevitably result in private conflicts, and the government must not be impotent to intervene in such circumstances. Critics, like Andrew Sullivan, the author of the controversial *Virtually Normal,* which makes the public neutrality case, might agree that the gay person should be granted *equality,* but argue that government neutrality, and nothing more, is the prescription. Even if this were a reasonable course, it is not a realistic one.

In his 1963 book, *Why We Can't Wait,* Martin Luther King Jr., relates, apropos of the African American civil rights struggle, a story about the efforts of the Jawaharlal Nehru government in bettering the lives of the untouchables, the lowest of the low in the Hindu caste system of India. Nehru admitted to King that many in India still harbored prejudice against the untouchables, but that it had become unpopular to exhibit these prejudices in any form. This was, in part, due to the moral example set by Mahatma Gandhi, but was also the cultural product of the Indian constitution, which specifically outlawed discrimination against the untouchables. Nehru told King that if two applicants competed for entrance to an Indian college or university, one applicant an untouchable and the other from the high caste, the institution was required by law to accept the untouchable. When Lawrence Reddick asked Nehru if that wasn't also discrimination, Nehru replied: "[T]his is our way of atoning for the centuries of injustices we have inflicted upon these people."[5]

I am not arguing for any system of quotas or preferences for gay Americans, such as King supported for African Americans, but I am saying that a mere statement of government neutrality isn't enough. At the least, we need antidiscrimination legislation in employment and housing. As King so adroitly states: "The struggle for rights is, at bottom, a struggle for opportunities."[6] What good, I ask, is the political enfranchisement of a minority—what good is a constitutional amendment granting a woman suffrage rights if she can be denied employment or housing based solely on the private biases arising from her public identity as a woman? Political enfranchisement means little when people cannot afford food or cannot acquire shelter. In cases in which discrimination has been so invidious for so long, as it has been with regard to African Americans, women, and gays in the United States, something more than a mere proclamation of governmental neutrality on the subject is needed to reverse ages of compounded injury. Why, I ask, should the principles that govern the relations between a liberal democracy and its members not also be expected to govern the relations among members of that democracy? Why, as Nehru suggested, when a government has been instrumental in establishing a society's discriminatory value sets and in coercing a minority to bow to those values without recourse, should it not also be instrumental in setting right the errors it previously compounded? What if we lived in a world in which there had been no Civil Rights Act of 1964, a world in which the American black was a voting citizen, but could still find no job, could still be capriciously denied housing, and could be refused service at any number of establishments with otherwise open access for the public? It would mean the development of a subculture that, in fact, did develop and that still lingers: the black ghetto. The world of the gay ghetto is not one in which I wish to live, but the ghetto would be the final stop for gays if government were to have no power to intervene in private discrimination resulting in ultimately public ramifications. Without these basic initial protections, gays can never be expected to arrive at the place of independence and self-assertiveness at which those, like Andrew Sullivan, who argue that protection from private discrimination goes too far, naively expect the gay person to begin. Those blighted by centuries of oppression simply cannot be expected to step undaunted into a world of unrestrained oppression. Government's interest in securing its citizens' civil rights is sometimes an interest in ensuring that those citizens behave *civilly* toward one another. These first steps are, I believe, necessary if there is to be hope for a transformation of the public's disposition toward and treatment of gays.

The supreme irony of politics is, of course, that its invariable end is to secure valued aspects of life outside politics. Most of the paramount battles of our political history have not been for the sake of politics itself; politics, instead, was a necessary means to a desired end. For example, most people would credit the Constitution's greatest accomplishment as the freedom it secures for us in our private lives and endeavors. Thus, if the aims of transformative politics are to become a reality, gays must take an active role and must urge sympathetic straights to take an active role in the radical redefinition of the public norms that continue to ensnare the American homosexual. The need for such activity is evident in our constitutional history, and I find it wholly appropriate and natural that the gay civil rights movement look for analogy and inspiration in the compelling movements that came before it.

Given the American proclivity to create hierarchies of human worth, it should not be surprising that the proper way to interpret the Constitution, as it bears on the status of any individual or group otherwise marginalized and disenfranchised, has been at the center of legal and political debate for the whole of American history. There are those who would have us believe that constitutional interpretation is something in the way of applied science, with precise, linear answers available by resort to one or another analytical formula, which are superior to any number of other such formulas. The idea, however, that constitutional interpretation is not, at its basest level, a question of politics or, more precisely, political philosophy, is erroneous. Justice Frankfurter admitted as much when he stated that constitutional interpretation "is not science, but applied politics."[7]

History's battles over constitutional interpretation and definition, while inevitably about something far greater than politics for politics' sake, have been waged through political channels. Take as an example the nineteenth-century battle for the abolition of slavery, which saw the use of politics as a necessary means to an end that ultimately meant more desirable and respectful public *and* private lives for American slaves. Although slavery certainly marks one of the darkest and most tragic periods in American history, it was also the precipitating factor of one of the greatest and furthest-reaching popular constitutional movements in U.S. history. The controversy surrounding slavery, from the moment it was arguably sanctioned by the Constitution, ultimately led to the American Civil War.

Even the poorest history student will know that the American Civil War ended slavery in the United States. But what is not well known (and what is particularly relevant and inspiring to the gay activist seeking to bring change) is the popular constitutionalism, the transformative politics, at work behind the scenes. The war, or, more precisely, the Thirteenth Amendment, ended slavery; but the immeasurable contributions by countless citizen abolitionists that preceded emancipation and citizenship for blacks should not be discounted. These contributions challenged a juridical conception of the Constitution that belied its overarching aspiration of human dignity and eventually redefined the constitutional norm of equality. They are important lessons for the gay activist—lessons about tenacity, perseverance, and, above all, the importance of responsible, attentive politics.

As assuredly as slavery bred popular unrest, it also bred bad law. The Supreme Court, for the better part of the nineteenth century, interpreted the Constitution to totally disenfranchise blacks. *Scott v. Sandford*, the infamous Dred Scott decision, marked one of the most pathetic moments in

American constitutional history. The Supreme Court effectively decided that slaves could not be citizens of the United States and invalidated the Missouri Compromise, which had checked the progression of slavery into new territory, with one bold sweep of the judicial pen. Yet, before and after Dred Scott, abolitionists campaigned against the ills of slavery and the debasement of constitutional morality that the courts too often embraced and fostered. The abolitionists understood that slavery did not comport with the Constitution's paramount precepts of human dignity and that any effort to legitimate the institution by constitutional reference inevitably would prove fruitless.

In the face of a contrary final word from the U.S. Supreme Court, it was the abolitionists' attack on the social ills of slavery and, more pointedly, their focus on the Constitution's mandates for humanity as a weapon against suppression of discourse and ultimately against slavery itself, that led to slavery's undoing in America. The abolitionists engaged in an analysis of American constitutionalism that went far beyond the Supreme Court's interpretation of what the Constitution said about slavery; they insisted that the Constitution demanded something entirely different. What they achieved is astonishing; most important, the abolitionists connected slavery to the greater ideals of the Constitution. The early abolitionist argument focused on a belief that all people have inalienable rights and that among these are the right to control their own bodies and persons, the right to free speech, and the right to acquire knowledge. In this way, the abolitionists reconnected America with the revolutionary roots of its constitutional reality. The abolitionists held as a fundamental tenet that the purpose of the Constitution was to reserve these rights from the ebb of political power; the aim of the abolitionists was that "the public mind" be "thoroughly revolutionized." Their criticisms of the prevailing constitutional interpretation and of the Constitution itself were strategically intended to stir the slavery controversy beyond constraint. Frederick Douglass proclaimed: "I hold that every American citizen has a right to form an opinion of the constitution, and to propagate that opinion, and to use all honorable means to make his opinion the prevailing one."[8] By refusing to consider himself intellectually bound by faulty interpretation or by the "final" decisions of the courts, Douglass realized and promoted the everyday role of the people in creating and redefining constitutional norms. Gays can learn much from the estimable examples of Douglass and the abolitionists, for gays, too, have a very real and important responsibility in shaping their own equality.

Likewise, the gay liberation movement faces many of the same hurdles that impeded the progress of the movement for woman's rights. Among them were bigoted, attenuated religious prejudices and decidedly bad law. Unfortunately for the American woman, the trilogy of post–American Civil War amendments that ostensibly brought equality to blacks preserved prejudices along gender lines. The Supreme Court, too, apparently had no regrets about perpetuating those biases. In the 1879 decision of *Strauder v. West Virginia*, the Court struck down a challenge by blacks to a West Virginia statute restricting jury service to whites only. The Court then added for good measure that the justices perceived no problem where the law restricted jury service to males only. In the early 1870s, the Court upheld laws that barred women from voting and from practicing law. In fact, it was not until the 1971 case of *Reed v. Reed* that the U.S. Supreme Court found a discriminatory gender-based classification unconstitutional.[9] This case was the beginning of successful constitutional litigation of women's rights claims. Popular constitutionalism was, however, at work well before the first positive stirrings in the Court. The National Organization for Women was formed in 1966, the National Association for the Repeal of Abortion Laws in 1969, and two other groups—the National Women's Political Caucus and the Women's Rights Project, which brought *Reed* to the Court—were formed in 1971.

The beginning of feminist organization, of course, far predates the advent of these groups. The earliest surge in feminist social development dates to Sarah and Angelina Grimké, sisters who rose to the challenge of gender inequality while laboring in the fight against slavery. The Grimké sisters, children of a slaveholder from South Carolina, migrated to Philadelphia, where they began to write and lecture for the abolitionist cause. By the late 1830s, the sisters were holding meetings in numerous New England towns. Although history today hails them as outspoken and successful advocates of both causes, they were met, in their own day, with stifling nineteenth-century convention that nearly silenced their efforts. Whereas religion (at least in the North) was often a powerful weapon in the abolitionist arsenal, it is surprising to find that religious convention was one of the greatest enemies of the Grimké sisters' abolitionist efforts. The South interpreted the dicta of Saint Paul to validate slavery, and Saint Paul was used in the North to invalidate the impassioned voices of the Grimké sisters.[10] The sisters' campaigning and foray into public life offended the prevailing religious sentiment of the day. The Council of Congregationalist Ministers of Massachusetts issued a staunch condemnation:

> We invite your attention to the dangers which at present seem to threaten the female character with widespread and permanent injury. The appropriate duties and influence of women are clearly stated in the New Testament. Those duties, and that influence are unobtrusive and private, but the sources of mighty power. When the mild, dependent, softening influence upon the sternness of man's opinions is fully exercised, society feels the effect of it in a thousand forms. The power of woman is her dependence, flowing from the consciousness of that weakness which God has given her for protection.[11]

Thus in seeking to contribute to the abolitionist cause, the sisters found that they were forced to fight a new battle.

But religious condemnation was not the only problem against which the Grimkés and their allies had to struggle. American law and religion were very much intertwined in the nineteenth century—as, indeed, they remain today. Perceived biblical biases against women had made their way into the American legal structure. The abolitionist cause was in full swing, and the increasingly anxious South looked for every way to quell the mounting chorus of antislavery sentiment. As abolitionist petitions from women's antislavery organizations poured into Congress, the House of Representatives passed the Pinckney Gag Rule to forbid their presentation. As Congressman Howard of Maryland declared, women, largely the petition gatherers, had no legal right to petition Congress, because they had no legal right to vote.

In 1848, when Elizabeth Cady Stanton, Lucretia Mott, and others met at Seneca Falls, New York, to draft the first petition for the redress of women's rights, a right to suffrage was inserted. Stanton quoted the Declaration of Independence and was supported by such notable popular constitutionalists as Frederick Douglass. Indeed, in 1894, Stanton boldly declared suffrage a natural right. The women argued that inequality for women challenged American revolutionary principles in the same way that slavery challenged them, and so needed to be abolished. The natural rights argument for the vote and the idea of the universality of the Declaration's principles, as they inform the Constitution, were arguments the woman's rights movement cultivated and utilized until the constitutional norm of equality was again changed—transformed—in 1920 and women were allowed to vote.

The gay rights movement, like any great American liberation movement, is about the same root constitutional question at issue in the movements recounted above: It is about the basic definition of constitutional equality. The results of the foregoing constitutional controversies may have surprised America's Founders, these men who countenanced slavery and disenfranchised women; but these Founders created a body of constitutional principles designed to be ever more fully recognized in the coming American era—in short, to surprise those mavericks whose immediate circumstances limited the vision of the constitutional order they created.

More broadly, the gay rights movement is about a seemingly limitless prejudice that permeates innumerable aspects of our public political life. Equality, the core concept of our American liberty, has proven to be a metabolic phenomenon, constantly changing as the value sets of the society shaping it, and shaped by it, change. Like the other great movements, the gay rights movement confronts the nation with the question whether that equality will be practiced to its fullest extent or whether it will be subordinated and subjugated to the religious and moral ideological views of those who find the biological definition of certain people unpalatable. The machinations of a moral majority, or even a powerful moral minority, of Americans, who withhold the golden promise of equality from a segment of their fellow Americans, are not a force easily reckoned with. Like the triumphant groups in previous paragraphs, gays need visionaries, luminaries, leaders, and sometimes seemingly superhuman feats of sacrifice and endurance. But they also need transformative politics, a basic human attentiveness to the political environment that ultimately will bring vindication.

Transformative politics might seem a curious invention. It does not have the same tenor of most of this century's political discussion. It does not answer when we ask which life is best or which undertaking noblest. Neither is it instantly a politic of redemption; it does not promise that every choice will yield desired results, nor does it promise that every sacrifice will be rewarded. But it is ultimately redemptive, for, like the political movements previously recounted, it is a politic that operates because of and within the human condition. At the heart of transformative politics lies the idea that no single response to the equality predicament is entirely accurate or tenable. Thus, there is a need to address various ideas and inquiries that affect the interplay of responsibility and gay politics (e.g., the coming out inquiry and a responsible, attentive look at the intermingling of religion and politics). These ideas are part of a political ecology forming the life of gay persons communally and individually.

This turning to attentiveness in realistic politics is a reclaiming of our dignity. No longer are we working against torture and medicalization; instead, we are working for respect and equality in society. Achieving respect through the promotion of genuine understanding and acceptance—as opposed to mere tolerance—will be the greatest achievement of the gay rights movement. Such achievement will come only through a responsible, attentive politics of action. For as surely as we are denied our dignity by bigots, censors, and zealots, we deny dignity to ourselves simply because we fail to assert our dignity, to work for it, to achieve it. Our vapid responses and interactions with the world around us do us little service in attaining the respect and recognition we deserve. The absence of politics serves only to defeat us.

Just as coming out is to be seen as a process rather than a movement, so too our politics is not a singular republican moment or legislative victory; rather our politics is a process of the evolving norms of a social ecology. Not so many years ago, the government did not have to explain its unequal treatment of gays, primarily because there was a social consensus that gays were degenerate, inverted, and predatory. That opinion was unfounded from the beginning and has more or less been obviated by a change in the collective social conscience. Much of that change, of course, should be credited to the countless courageous gay men and women who have come out of the closet over time.

Our struggle has been both moral and legislative. We may take as a paradigm the debate over same-sex marriage. The Supreme Judicial Court of Massachusetts has ordered that same-sex marriages—not civil unions or domestic partnerships, but marriages—go forward in that state. It has been a long and arduous road. The legislators of Massachusetts, along with legislators in numerous other states and the national Congress, now grapple with how to come to terms with the court's decree. Transformative politics is needed now more than ever. Opponents and supporters of gay marriage recognize that the debate is about much more than memoranda and bills; same sex-marriage is part of a far greater normative debate in America. No mere legal technicality is here at issue, but the fate of time-honored and valorized

ethical norms, mores, and communitarian value sets: Compulsory heterosexuality is losing its primacy.

Consequently, the serious arguments against same-sex marriage can all
be seen as arguments about the public good. William Eskridge astutely sum-
marizes the arguments as follows: First, the ultimate good of marriage is procreation; thus there can be no right of same-sex marriage, as it is
oxymoronic; second, same-sex marriage would constitute state promotion
of a union ultimately detrimental to partners and children; third, gay
unions would undermine heterosexual marriage. The actual content of
these arguments is less important than the realization that they are all public, communal arguments. The very nature of the debate is what is edifying,
instructing gays to move from their ideas about the privacy of their relationships to the very public reality of what their relationships mean on the
national scene.

It is insisted that the common good of marriage is that of sexual unions,
legitimized by marriage and resulting in procreation. The arguments are, of
course, circular. Traditionalists assert the procreative good as the only conceivable good of marriage, and critics deny it to be so. The very public nature of the debate, however, cannot be denied, and a gay withdrawal to the
privacy realm leaves damaging public assertions unanswered. One such
painful assertion is that gays are promiscuous and spread diseases, such as
HIV/AIDS. Now, a rational reply is that one cannot fault the gay person for
promiscuity and then deny that person the very vehicle by which others
have traditionally entered settled, monogamous relationships. Too often,
however, the reply is an off-center assertion that what one does in his or her
bedroom is his or her own business. There is truth in that statement, but it
is the wrong response.

The assertion that children somehow need defending is another oft-
heard chorus. Gays, it is argued, harm children because they inevitably engage in extramarital conduct that will set an immoral example. It is also
argued that gay unions confuse children about gender roles. The idea that
gay couples will put sexual gratification ahead of a child's welfare is unfounded. The plaintiffs in *Baker v. Vermont,* the case establishing the first
state civil union system, began litigation chiefly because they were concerned about the welfare and future security of their son. Moreover, studies
suggest that the ills proffered by gay marriage opponents are not well-
founded concerns. Assertions of molestation add a bitter icing to the absurd
cake. Eskridge aptly calls it a "politics of preservation with a hard edge."[12]

These public arguments quickly degenerate into bigoted expressions that strike at the very core of the gay individual—but the arguments remain powerfully public. The private and public are inextricably intertwined.

This is a politic of public preservation perhaps best summarized by the argument contending that the legalization of gay marriage will somehow undermine heterosexual marriage. Massachusetts will do much to underscore the falsity of this argument. Gay couples have married and continue to marry, and the sky has not fallen. The idea that two people in a loving, committed relationship could do anything other than enhance the common good is an increasingly transparent fallacy. What should be clear from these arguments, of course, is that they are about public status, the preservation of heterosexual hegemony, and the continued encroachment of religion into American political life.

Gays cannot allow these dangerous suppositions to go unanswered. But how does one answer such tainted, seemingly inexorable arguments? The answer, I believe, lies in transformative politics, which encompasses a continued public reasoning in the face of morally speculative argument. And transformative politics, in one form or another, has been effective. In the past century, every state made homosexuality a felony or otherwise criminal offense. The gay person was brutalized, politically marginalized, and shoved into a pariah caste. Yet, today, our country, reformed by decades of gay activism, has changed. No longer is the innate sexual expression of the gay person criminalized. No longer will overt and otherwise baseless discriminatory action against the gay person be widely tolerated. While gay people are still treated reprehensibly in many respects, as the marriage amendment controversy underscores, things have changed in undeniably positive ways through a transformative political ethic; not to admit this would be as destructive as blindly ignoring the labors still left to pursue. Transformative politics ultimately will carry the day because its demand for equality inevitably trumps the self-interested traditional arguments. Progress, however, remains slower than otherwise possible because gay activism is stunted by the inertia of the closet and the closet's focus on the private domain. Gays remain substantially underorganized, inactive, and ineffective; consequently, we might be part of the American community, but we are not yet equal citizens.

Just as the planned gradualism of the assimilationists will not work, neither will the unplanned assertion of immediate full equality necessarily be productive. The gay person must be open to a politic of evolutionary progression. As gay opponents have said, they do not want gay equality "shoved down their throats." Instead, gay politics must be a politic of conditioning and transformation. That is why I have written about the importance to the movement of visibility and of coming out. Coming out plants the seed of future transformation, but it makes no unyielding counterproductive demands. This is not to suggest that we should follow the line of the gay right, who suggest that we circumscribe our inquietude and give sympathetic straight Americans time to change themselves. God knows they have had time enough to change of their own accord; gays have been the scapegoats for straight America's private insecurities for too long; they have been the sacrifice to appease a puritanical God and to atone for the inevitable failure to live up to his precepts. But the curious thing about scapegoats is that, after all the bloodletting, the sacrifice fails to redeem the sinner, and the whole horrendous cycle is left to be repeated. To break the cycle, gays need a calculated, sometimes cautious, involvement in urging change for the better.

Exactly how to go about securing our equal place in society is a matter of the greatest significance. Like most matters of great import, this one has few uncomplicated answers. Supposing to know the future of gay rights in America is a precarious endeavor; change is rushing onto the American scene at a dizzying pace; yet this is an important, ineluctable speculation. The direction of our future politics of action must be guided not only by an understanding of historical injustices but also by an examination of the obstacles we currently face and will face in the future. Some of these, like the effect of religious interest groups, have been discussed at length already; what follows is a discussion of the current sociopolitical framework in which our politics must operate.

At any given point in the history of a society, the policies and resolutions of any given controversy can be understood as functions of the attitudes of a continuum of differing, yet overlapping, constituencies. Naturally, the power to set public policy is not distributed equally among these groups. Anyone who hopes to change policy for the better must be able to identify the constituencies involved in the power play in order to find some leverage or influence in favor of the preferred policy of a progression to full equality.

The following discussion is certainly not exhaustive, but it is a useful exposé to understanding the current status of gays as well as possible future developments in the arena of gay equality in the United States. The discussion is designed to identify and outline those institutions of American public life that are intimately involved in antigay politics as well as those most sympathetic and desirous of a move toward equality. This discussion is ultimately necessary to understanding the hurdles faced by those embracing the responsibilities of gay citizenship previously outlined.

THE RELIGIOUS RIGHT . . .

To those who have read this book from the beginning it is evident that a significant portion of this work has been devoted to the discussion of the role of religious fundamentalism in the construction and perpetuation of antigay bias and homophobia. It should come as no surprise, then, that the most powerful and successful obstacle to gay advancement has been the religious right (in this instance, I include the Roman Catholic Church along with America's evangelical fundamentalist tradition).

The Roman Catholic Church has moved from a relatively benign position of viewing homosexuality as a non-sinful orientation (although it has maintained, at least since the Middle Ages, that homosexual sex acts were sinful and in later times that the orientation was "disordered") to, most recently, an all-inclusive condemnation of homosexuality of any kind. In the wake of the *Lawrence v. Texas* decision by the U.S. Supreme Court, the Vatican issued a statement in which it decreed that the mere exposure of young children to homosexuals is tantamount to child abuse. Additionally, in response to the foundation-rocking child abuse scandals in the United States, the Vatican has sought to strengthen its earlier teachings about sex, including the subordination of women in the church, the innate evils of contraception, and, of course, the refusal to recognize homosexuality as anything but unnatural and contrary to divine design. The Vatican has finally taken its own views on homosexuality out of the closet, articulating that its former "love gays, hate homosexuality" mantra was really a thinly veneered coverup of a more strident hatred of gays themselves. Shortly after the child abuse scandal broke, Bishop Wilton Gregory, head of the Conference of Catholic Bishops in the United States, the American church's resident governing body, said that the problem of pederasty within the church was essentially a problem of homosexuals in the church—a statement that, quite naturally, sent shockwaves through America's gay community. The Pope's spokesman, Joaquin Navarro-Valls, is on record as stating: "People with these inclinations just cannot be ordained."[13] And the war has begun.

The gay priesthood is a very real worry to the Vatican. A study of the priesthood commissioned by the bishops in the 1980s, and then quickly aborted, found these traits in seminarians (as summarized by Richard Sipe):

Dependency—a tendency to depend on others for direction and validation.

Little interest in the opposite sex.

An emphasis on aesthetic interests over athletic or mechanical pastimes.

An idealized view of women (mother dominance).[14]

To the extent that these findings can be said to reflect homosexual orientation, at least in males, they are indicative of the gay presence in the clergy. I am not suggesting that all gay males possess or exhibit these traits; I am simply suggesting, along with Sipe, that these stereotypical gay traits are exhibited, to some degree, by homosexuals who are, or would be, attracted to the priesthood. This was evidently also the conclusion of the Catholic bishops, for the study promptly was canceled when its direction became apparent.

Recent surveys of seminarians find large numbers who describe their seminaries as "predominantly gay."[15] In the preceding two decades, large numbers of heterosexual priests have resigned from the priesthood in the face of the church's continued refusal to entertain the concept of a married clergy—even though, as many proponents argue, this prohibition did not exist in the early church. Even among those heterosexuals who remained in the priesthood the idea that a married priesthood should be permitted by Rome and an overall openness to the various manifestations of human sexuality have created an environment in which gays have felt more able to consider and acknowledge their own sexuality. Gay authors like John Boswell (*Christianity, Social Tolerance, and Homosexuality*) and John McNeill, a former priest, (*The Church and the Homosexual*) have produced hugely influential works on the nature and naturalness of homosexuality, evidently particularly influential among American clergy. Among American Catholics, already almost Protestant in the selectivity with which they approach the Vatican's teachings, there is a strong trend afoot to read the passages of condemnation, especially those of St. Paul, which seem to be the most relevant to the modern Christian, as having been condemnations, like those of Philo, of pederasty, not as general condemnations of homosexuality. It is interesting to note that, as a Catholic and weekly mass attendee for nearly a decade, I have yet to sit through a homily on the evils of homosexuality. This is not to say that such sermons are not preached. In April 2002, Monsignor Eugene Clark, stepping in for the embattled Cardinal Egan (who has been disparaged for looking the other way when confronted with evidence of pedophile priests) preached a blistering attack on homosexuality in New York's St. Patrick's Cathedral. Curiously, though, Clark aimed his accusations of disorder only at priests, not naming the countless bishops and other irresolute superiors who did incalculable damage by covering up pedophilia within the church—another example of hierarchical scapegoating.

The easing of biases within the churches, if not at the Vatican, has had other effects. For example, in addition to those priests who withdrew from the priesthood because of the Vatican's recalcitrance on the issue of marriage, some homophobic heterosexual men doubtlessly have withdrawn from the seminary or avoided seminaries altogether. Thus, although the Vatican's attenuations of pederasty with homosexuality remain absurd, there may be some validity to the Vatican's fears that a proliferation of gays in the priesthood ultimately may threaten the already diminishing ranks of the priesthood. Ironically, the Vatican's recent crackdown on gay seminarians and seminary hopefuls may hasten the equally detested (by the Vatican) prospect of a married clergy; otherwise, with the sizable number of gays driven out of the priesthood, there finally may be too few priests to pastor America's Catholic community.

Gays in the priesthood may threaten the Pope's obdurate refusal to loosen the clerical obligation of celibacy. As Garry Wills points out in his book, *Papal Sin*, a significant number of surveyed priests think that celibacy means "not being married to a woman—a definition that would make all single gay men, even the most promiscuous, celibate."[16] Again, as discontent with and disregard for the mandate of celibacy gain in fervor, the Vatican may be forced either to rely on the gay priests or to cave on its marriage requirements. Feeling forced to choose among these abominations is what frightens the theological conservatives within the church's hierarchy.

Consequently, although the threat may be a threat forced by senseless rules, gay priests and gays generally constitute a menace to the Vatican's sacrosanct status quo, and the Vatican has circled its wagons. Its more recent, scathing attacks on gays and homosexuality are manifestations of a church running scared.[17]

The same can be said of the other component of fundamentalism I have already discussed at length in this book, fundamentalist Protestantism. Protestant fundamentalists in this country have been masterful in the promotion of their antigay agenda. Whereas the Catholic Church has just begun to attempt an exercise of overt control over public officials who stray over doctrinal lines (e.g., the refusal of some bishops to allow presidential candidate John Kerry to receive communion because of his anti-Vatican stance on abortion and other controversial issues in the 2004 election [of course, they have the embodiment of the Catholic conservative on the Supreme Court, Justice Scalia, and thanks to Scalia's son, a priest, the Court is now blessed with two Catholic arch-conservatives, for Father Scalia helped convert Clarence Thomas to Catholicism in 1997—to think, Jefferson and Adams opposed even the presence of the Jesuits in America]), Protestant fundamentalists have built and maintained for decades now extraordinarily effective political machines. In fact, before the Vatican's switch to a more active role in the antigay campaign, gay rights opposition was chiefly the province of brasher Protestant fundamentalist sects. They have been masterfully organized and well funded. Numerous groups, the successors of groups like the Moral Majority and the Christian Coalition, are adept at using the Republican Party as a vehicle for legislating their religiously based antigay policies.

The fundamentalist campaign against the progression of gay rights is one component in a comprehensive social agenda built around the fundamentalists' primary perception of a traditional social order threatened from all sides. This wary pessimism has been the key to the survival of the fundamentalist sects since their emergence in force early in the twentieth century in response to the eclipse of agrarian America by urbanization and the systematic breakdown of social and sexual taboos in the wake of that modernization. They constitute a particularly strident and effective voice in favor of keeping gays in subjugated positions—primarily because they believe that such a cultural assault is biblically based. Because of their adherence to what they believe to be biblical injunction, an effort on the part of gays to assert their whole personhood through military service or marital rights is not merely something unpalatable or inappropriate; it is to be warred against as the potential undoing of civilization.

The success of their campaign has ebbed—Jerry Falwell's popularity took a considerable hit when he began to delve too deeply into politics to suit some of his followers. In recent years, he has returned, withdrawn from the center of controversy to some degree, but even this has not kept him from taking a jab at gays when the opportunity arises—not the least of which was his 2001 decree that the 9/11 terrorist attacks were God's punishment for America's growing acceptance of homosexuality (and feminism). Falwell was joined in this pronouncement by Pat Robertson, who has perhaps become more of a political figure than a religious one. Robertson even has been a Republican presidential contender.

Although they may be in agreement about the sinful nature of homosexuality, not all fundamentalists have seen fit to enter the political fray. For many, the paramount mission of saving souls takes precedence over culture war. Even in these communities, being identified as an opponent of gay rights has consequences, as charges of bigotry and homophobia are becoming more and more common.

POLITICAL PARTIES . . .

For many years, there has been an ideological division concerning gay rights in which the Republican Party has been the party opposed to gay rights progression. This division can be explained most plausibly by the GOP being beholden to religious interest groups, particularly those of the evangelical fundamentalist right. Evangelical voters are responsible for substantial amounts of funding to Republican candidates and the party itself, who they believe will further their religious-based agendas. They are also remarkably motivated voters, often turning out to the polls because of an abiding, obsessive interest in one or two issues pertinent to an election, for example, abortion and gay rights. There are, of course, aberrations, with the Log Cabin Republicans, a gay Republican anomaly, being most notable. There has been dissension in the ranks of even a group such as this, however, given the Republican Party's—particularly President Bush's—support for a federal marriage amendment that not only would settle the question of marriage at the federal level but also would strip states of the ability to decide the question of same-sex marriage within their own jurisdictions. Notwithstanding, it should be understood that the gay Republican movement might be a little self-delusional. The Log Cabin Republicans of Texas were denied a booth at the party's 2004 national convention (in which they supported George W. Bush, former governor of Texas) because of their gay rights advocacy and were set upon by a mob of counter-protestors, many of them Republican delegates.

The Democratic Party, by contrast, has not taken as forceful a position regarding gay rights. While it is true that the Democratic Party is the party most receptive, in general, to pleas by gay constituencies and that it has been so impugned by the Republican Party, the Democrats' record of consistency is unimpressive. The last president produced by the Democrats, Bill Clinton, ran on a platform that called for the lifting of the ban on gays in the military. Clinton, however, caved under pressure from Republicans and other interests and disappointed many gays by adopting the compromise "don't ask, don't tell" policy. Clinton also supported the federal Defense of Marriage Act (DOMA), which sought to obviate the interstate recognition of gay unions in the wake of Hawaii's near recognition of same-sex marriage. Clinton did, however, do more for gay rights than any president in history, removing difficulties in security clearances, changing the federal bureaucracy to prohibit discrimination in employment, and escalating the AIDS war.

Whether it is the choice of a lesser evil or a true belief in the political platform, gays tend to be most supportive of the Democratic Party. According to a June 25, 1996, *Advocate* article, Bill Clinton got some 75 percent of the gay vote and $3.5 million in financing. Gays also overwhelmingly supported Al Gore in his election bid against George W. Bush. Gore, however, had a shakier track record on gay issues; in the 1970s, he was an anti-gay voice. Although gay groups looked on him as reformed through his association with the Clinton administration, Gore said that he did not favor gay marriage. He did, however, favor immigration rights for foreigners engaged in same-sex relationships with American citizens and a lifting of the ban on gays in the military.

Politicians themselves have a difficult tightrope walk to perform when it comes to issues of gay rights. Today, as the terms "homophobe" and "bigot" are applied with more frequency, politicians can less often risk a public attack on gays. But they also cannot risk alienating the powerful conservative, Christian right voting block. When running for president, Bill Clinton found himself arguing for the extension of gay rights but not the "promotion of the homosexual lifestyle." Likewise, when pressed for his views on homosexuality in a hypothetical situation about his having a gay grandchild, George H. W. Bush stammered to come up with his answer, which called for compassion and understanding for the child but made certain not to convey the message that homosexuality was an "acceptable lifestyle." "I'd love that child," he said. "I would put my arms around him. I would hope he wouldn't go out and try to convince people that this was a normal lifestyle, that this was an appropriate lifestyle, that this was the way to be. But I would say, 'I hope you don't become an advocate for a lifestyle that in my view is not normal, and propose marriage, same-sex marriages as a normal way of life.'"[18]

The vermiculations of the politicians in these examples demonstrate that homosexuality is a potentially explosive political issue no matter how it is handled. Like abortion and the death penalty, gay rights perhaps ought not to be an issue over which political parties schism; but it is such an issue in the United States. As it is, there is little hope that even the more liberal Democratic Party will throw its unreserved support behind the issue(s) of gay rights. What we can hope, however, is that the Democrats, unlike the Republicans, will not use gays as political punching bags to demonstrate their toughness on family values (or as columnist Liz Smith put it, perhaps more accurately, "family values junk").

LEGISLATURES . . .

The status of gay rights begins and often ends with the legislature, be it the U.S. Congress or the general assemblies of the several states. Of course, much of the legislative effect on gays and gay rights can be summed up by the observations made in the previous section discussing political parties. Legislators and their legislation are often the products of heavily entrenched ideological party differences. Much good that has come by way of court decision has been undone or severely compromised by legislative action.

Most disturbing is the proposed Federal Marriage Amendment. Introduced by Senator A. Wayne Allard (R) of Colorado in March 2004, obviously in direct response to fears ignited or intensified by the *Lawrence* decision, the Senate version of the amendment reads:

Marriage in the United States shall consist only of the union of a man and a woman. Neither this Constitution, nor the constitution of any State, shall be construed to require that marriage or the legal incidents thereof be conferred upon any union other than the union of a man and a woman.[19]

When considered on July 14, 2004, the Senate version failed to garner even a simple majority, let alone the two-thirds vote required by the Constitution.

The House version, introduced by Representative Marilyn Musgrave (R) of Colorado in May 2003 reads as follows:

> Marriage in the United States shall consist only of the union of a man and a woman. Neither this Constitution nor the constitution of any State, nor state or federal law, shall be construed to require that the marital status or the legal incidents thereof be conferred upon unmarried couples or groups.[20]

The idea that the Constitution should be amended to limit individual liberty and even to circumscribe the nearly sacrosanct doctrine of state's rights is testament to the degree of influence of the religious right.

Similarly, the federal Defense of Marriage Act (DOMA), signed by President Clinton on September 21, 1996, reads:

> In determining the meaning of any Act of Congress, or of any ruling, regulation, or interpretation of the various administrative bureaus and agencies of the United States, the word 'marriage' means only a legal union between one man and one woman as husband and wife, and the word 'spouse' refers only to a person of the opposite sex who is a husband or a wife.[21]

State legislatures have enacted state DOMAs. The *Goodridge* decision extending the availability of civil marriage to gays in Massachusetts is also vulnerable to legislative override. In 2004, both houses of the Massachusetts legislature met and passed a constitutional amendment requiring marriage to be between one man and one woman but making civil unions available for same-sex couples. The amendment, however, failed to pass a joint session of the legislature in the 2005–6 term, which would have allowed the amendment to go to voters for ratification. The text as passed in 2004 reads:

> The unified purpose of this Article is both to define the institution of civil marriage and to establish civil unions to provide same-sex persons with entirely the same benefits, protections, rights, privileges and

obligations as are afforded to married persons, while recognizing that under present federal law benefits same-sex [*sic*] persons in civil unions will be denied federal benefits available to married persons.

It being the public policy of this Commonwealth to protect the unique relationship of marriage, only the union of one man and one woman shall be valid or recognized as a marriage in the Commonwealth.

Two persons of the same sex shall have the right to form a civil union if they otherwise meet the requirements set forth by law for marriage. Civil unions for same-sex persons are established by the Article and shall provide entirely the same benefits, protections, rights, privileges and obligations that are afforded to persons married under the law of the Commonwealth. All laws applicable to marriage shall also apply to civil unions.[22]

Several inconsistencies should be evident to the reader. First, the Massachusetts legislature is taking great pains to preserve the heterocentric, theocentric term "marriage." Thus, while purporting to bestow all of the benefits of marriage to gay couples, the amendment's civil union compromise automatically relegates gays to second-class status. Second, after this insult, the legislature goes on to state that, to be eligible for a civil union, a gay couple must meet the requirements for a marriage under Massachusetts law. The absurdity of requiring a couple to meet the requirements of marriage and then arbitrarily denying them a marriage cannot be overstated. The Massachusetts legislature has underscored the irrationality of a marriage/civil union distinction. The ultimate impact of this sort of legislative action on the legal and social status of gays remains to be seen, but it is obviously potentially devastating.[23]

Here, I especially would like to note that the amendment points out the undeniably religious underpinnings of the effort to "protect" marriage by separating it from another status—civil union—that might be conceded to gays. Efforts like those of the Massachusetts legislature (to confer all the benefits and responsibilities of marriage, while avoiding the actual term), underscore the religious nature of the argument. The argument of President Bush (who, after the votes of American evangelicals were safely cast in the 2004 election, endorsed a more "compassionate conservative" version of the Federal Marriage Amendment that would leave the civil union avenue open to the states) and others is that the status of marriage should be kept intact as a union of a man and a woman because of the traditional religious connotations the term evokes. This is problematic because government passes judgment on the religious appropriateness of various forms of marriage purely out of a desire to protect a prevailing sectarian ideology. If the nonestablishment norm of the First Amendment to the U.S. Constitution means anything, it should mean that government is prohibited from passing just this kind of religious-based judgment.

Moreover, a growing number of religious denominations and groups (some American Episcopal churches, the United Church of Christ, some meetings of the Fellowship of Friends, the Unitarian/Universalists, some independent Baptists, the Metropolitan Community Church, and others) now include the blessing of same-sex unions (but for the denial of a civil marriage license, I could call them marriages) as part of their *agape* love message. Under these circumstances, we might say that governmental action to restrict access to marriage is either an establishment of the countervailing religious preference regarding marriage, a hindrance of the *agape* churches' right to free religious exercise (also guaranteed by the First Amendment), or both. Perhaps government would be better off, and certainly more constitutionally sound, were it to distance itself from any sacramental definition of marriage and to focus on its legitimate interest, the conferring of benefits. If government has decided, as it has and probably has a right to do, that the right to certain benefits will be triggered for individuals only once they have entered a marriage partnership, perhaps government would be better off issuing "civil unity" licenses, as opposed to "marriage licenses." It could thereby keep track of relationships triggering certain benefits without becoming bogged down in the morass of disagreement over the proper sectarian definition of marriage.

Conversely, if the institution of marriage is now sufficiently secularized that it no longer involves these sectarian identity issues (which I doubt), then I can discern no truly secular purpose, as most religious liberties scholars would agree is required by the First Amendment's nonestablishment norm, for perpetuating a distinction between marriage and some other form of union. In this case, the distinction should be eradicated.

This is a line of reasoning not likely to convince the current Supreme Court, but it is, nevertheless, reasoning that should be considered by the responsible law or policy maker, as well as the voting citizen, who is also a person of faith.

THE COURTS . . .

The courts have been both the greatest asset and the greatest stumbling block to gay and lesbian rights in this country. *Bowers v. Hardwick* was a constitutional blight ranking with the Supreme Court's backing of the World War II internment of Japanese Americans or its pronouncement of "separate but equal" accommodations for African Americans. But then there is *Lawrence*, the furthest expansion of gay and lesbian rights at the federal level.

The Constitution has proven to be a powerful defense for gays and lesbians in this country. Certainly, a major component of the constitutional right to privacy is the right of individuals to live their lives free of unwarranted governmental interference. This is precisely what the Court denied gays in *Bowers v. Hardwick*, and what Justice John Paul Stevens recognized in his dissent as "embod[ying] the moral fact that a person belongs to himself and not others nor to society as a whole." The *Bowers* decision was assailed by scholars and civil libertarians from the moment pen touched paper. In the interim between *Bowers* and *Lawrence v. Texas*, the state courts were filling the rights void created by *Bowers*. State courts, exemplified by the Kentucky Supreme Court in *Kentucky v. Wasson*, began to recognize that the legal marginalization of gays based on ignorance and irrational biases was incompatible with the democratic ideal and was not constitutionally sustainable. Finally, in *Lawrence*, the U.S. Supreme Court, too, recognized a federal constitutional right to privacy for gays and lesbians and overruled *Bowers*. Justice Anthony Kennedy, writing for the majority, opined that "[sodomy laws] demean the lives of homosexual persons . . . [and homosexuals] are entitled to respect for their private lives."[24]

Although not all courts have looked upon gays favorably (the North Carolina Supreme Court undid favorable precedent in the 1990s when it ruled in the case of *Pulliam v. Smith* that a parent's homosexuality, without a showing of harm to the child, was a negative factor in custody considerations), most substantial victories in the gay causes—notably gay marriage—have come by way of the judiciary. The first stirrings in the gay union movement came in 1993, when the Hawaii Supreme Court ruled that Hawaii's restriction of marriage to opposite-sex couples would be presumed unconstitutional unless the state could demonstrate that it furthered a compelling state interest. The Hawaii court decision was overridden by a state constitutional amendment, as was a similar decree by the Alaska high court in 1998. *Baker v. Vermont*, the case that legalized civil unions in the state of Vermont, is another example of judicial deliberation yielding favorable results for the gay and lesbian community. In November 2003, the Supreme Judicial Court of Massachusetts, in *Goodridge v. Department of Public Health*, ruled that denying marriage licenses to gay and lesbian couples violated the equality and liberty guarantees of the Massachusetts constitution.

The constitutional promise of equal protection requires that legally inequitable treatment of a group of people must be based on something more substantive and legitimate than a prevailing popular prejudice. Although the move from *Bowers* to *Lawrence* shows the slow and wounding progression to judicial vindication, the courts remain the most powerful weapon in the gay and lesbian arsenal against oppression and unequal treatment.

CIVIL LIBERTIES AND CIVIL RIGHTS GROUPS . . .

Since the Mattachine Society of the 1950s, beleaguered gays have coalesced into groups in pursuit of the strength in number truism and to offer the world a more univocal and well-organized response to prejudice and bigotry. Certainly, and as one might expect, the American Civil Liberties Union (ACLU) has been involved in the support of gay rights for many years. But in recent decades, there has been a rise of more gaycentric civil rights movements. Gays have been relatively successful in the fusion of interest group politics with radicalism and have achieved no small feats in the redefinition of sex and sexuality in this country. In the 1980s and early 1990s, the activist group, AIDS Coalition to Unleash Power (ACT UP) did much to bring needed attention to the plight of AIDS patients. During the extremely homophobic Reagan and George H. W. Bush administrations, little was done by the government in the way of AIDS response. It was an issue simply overlooked in favor of more politically palatable planks in the platform, like the so-called War on Drugs. Meanwhile, countless Americans and untold numbers abroad were ravaged by AIDS. ACT UP challenged the status quo and, far from merely asking for it, they demanded attention.

ACT UP's methods—shrill confrontation whenever possible (Larry Kramer, the founder of ACT UP, called George H. W. Bush a murderer)— were criticized by some as rash and even counterproductive. Nevertheless, ACT UP's accomplishments should not be diminished. ACT UP gave AIDS and the lack of proper governmental response the visibility needed.

ACT UP also took on the Catholic Church for its indurate response to the pandemic—particularly its insistence that condom use is sinful.

Other organizations like Queer Nation and the Rainbow Coalition (in response to the Christian Coalition) have had varying degrees of success. Generally, they have proven to be fast-burning wicks, their missions becoming quickly disorganized and degenerating into chaos.

For many people, the Human Rights Campaign (HRC) is more palatable, from a standpoint of decorum, in its tactics to bring gay issues to the political forefront and to promote equality. The HRC has emerged as the most successful and respected gay rights group in its efforts promoting AIDS research, domestic partnership legislation, hate crime legislation, and employment antidiscrimination policy. Recently, the HRC has taken on its most monumental work in the fight to defeat the misbegotten federal marriage amendment. The completion of an impressive national headquarters in Washington, D.C., in 2003 marks the HRC as a sustained and formidable presence on the political landscape.

Other organizations, like the Gay and Lesbian Alliance Against Defamation (GLAAD), have been successful in changing, to some degree, the way in which gays are depicted on television and reported in the news. If visibility is the key to rights progression, some attention surely must be given to the kind of visibility garnered. GLAAD has done much to ensure that gays and lesbians are not brutalized by broadcasters and that the quality of the visibility is as good as can be hoped.

THE MEDIA . . .

Books on gay subjects and themes flow forth from the presses in unprecedented numbers, more often than not from authors supportive of equal rights for gays and lesbians in the United States. Recent monographs deriding the gay rights movement are virtually unknown. Yet serious scholarship about gay rights is not the source from which most Americans draw their limited knowledge about gay people and gay people's lives. The print media, in the form of newspapers and news magazines, have given the gay rights movement lukewarm response. Major papers typically recognized as having a liberal bent, like the *New York Times* or the *Los Angeles Times*, while far from being overtly hostile to gays, often have given gays and gay-centric issues marginal reportage. The two-week-long 1991 demonstrations following California Governor Pete Wilson's turncoat veto of important antidiscrimination legislation were covered as a virtual footnote by leading papers, including even the *Los Angeles Times*.

The portrayal of happy lesbians and gay men in sustained, long-term relationships is dangerous to the heterosexual culture monopoly because it debunks the myth that gays are inevitably lonely, isolated, and unhappy. Consequently, representations of gays in the popular media were virtually unknown prior to the 1970s, and, when finally represented in the 1970s, gays were invariably depicted as isolated and despondent. In the 1980s and 1990s, the ravages of the AIDS pandemic brought gays into the media spotlight, but in even this broader coverage, death was synonymous with homosexuality, and America's Calvinists harped on "the wages of sin." Even when more favorable representations did come along, there was concerted effort to keep them out of the mainstream. Neoconservative cultural critic Bruce Bawer was terminated as movie reviewer for the conservative magazine *American Spectator* for refusing to alter a piece in which he favorably reviewed a play, *Prelude to a Kiss*, and a film, *Longtime Companion*, (both works by the same writer-director team) that dared sympathetically to portray gays as ordinary.

Also disturbing was the coverage afforded the outing controversy of the 1990s, in which journalists like Michelangelo Signorile set about exposing the secret gay lives of public figures, including that of a high-ranking Bush administration official, Pete Williams, in order to draw attention to the hypocrisy of the institutionalized closet. Their efforts were met with vitriolic opposition by the so-called mainstream press. Signorile's efforts were branded McCarthyism by the media, reinforcing the idea that to be identified as a homosexual was as bad as being identified as a communist in the 1950s. The media, either obtusely or intentionally, missed the point—that accusations of homosexuality could destroy the lives and careers of targets—and that this went to the heart of what is wrong with the closet and current societal treatment of gays and lesbians. They preferred to sugarcoat the issue for their readers and to focus on admonishing gay rights activists to use more civil tactics.

Perhaps worst of all in terms of fair treatment of gay and lesbian issues are the visual media. Gays and lesbians are now a media presence in a way that seemed unthinkable just five years ago. Certainly, this visibility has done much to advance the gay rights cause. And yet, something must be said about the kind of visibility afforded gays. Generally, any role afforded gay characters is one centered entirely on their sexuality and completely obscuring any other human aspects. Often, the gay person is portrayed as silly and frivolous, with silly and frivolous concerns.

But more disturbing than the treatment of gays in the entertainment media, is the treatment given them in the news media. As in other aspects of society, the complete sexualization of the gay person in the news media is also ultimately his victimization. I remember vividly the sensational coverage given to the Jeffrey Dahmer trial in the 1990s. Dahmer's horrific acts of murder and cannibalism were diminished, somehow lost, in the media's focus on the sexual orientation of killer and prey. There was an "asked for it" element in the coverage that outraged many gays.

Still, the media remain the most utilitarian vehicle for gays to publish their message. It is unnerving for many gays to be asked by the media to answer the same old questions and to refute the same old biases. But this is a necessary tool in the movement toward equality. An effective, organized use of the media can be a powerful weapon against ignorance, as exemplified by the use of local media by local and state gay rights groups as well as national groups like the Human Rights Campaign, who recently profiled longtime committed gay couples in short spots intended to counter the silly contention that gays neither want nor are capable of monogamy. As our world becomes ever more televised, the importance of effective utilization of the media will prove to be a key in the gay rights movement.

BUSINESS AND INDUSTRY . . .

Although the business community does not immediately leap to mind when one thinks of gay rights opposition, it has played some role in the circumvention of gay rights initiatives over the years. For example, in my home state of North Carolina, the business community in the city of Raleigh objected loudly when gay rights advocates attempted to extend the protections of a nondiscrimination ordinance, previously applying to government only, to the private sector. Corporations also have been opposed to HIV initiatives that would result in corporate financial burden. Typically, however, as with the Raleigh example, most business community opposition to gay rights comes at the small business level. Often, as was the case in Raleigh, business owners simply motivate the preexisting animus of grassroots evangelical groups in order to accomplish their ends at the electoral level.

THE GAY POLITICAL RIGHT . . .

We cannot leave a discussion of obstacles in the path of gay equality without examining the curious rise of the gay right. The 1980s and 1990s saw the emergence of a conservative gay interest that has systematically criticized the work of the gay liberation movement. Those individuals comprising the gay right, personified by the likes of Bruce Bawer and Andrew Sullivan, are wont to brand any manifestation of dissent not fitting the heterosexual paradigm as subculture and counterproductive. But these, even these, are out gay men. The most insidious segment of the gay right are those who live clandestinely, while working for bigots and homophobes for their own self-gain and ultimately degrading themselves and their fellow gays, like Arthur Finkelstein, the Republican political strategist who worked for such hateful opponents as Senators Jesse Helms and Lauch Faircloth, all while living with his partner and their adopted children in closeted deceit.

The hostility between gays at opposite ends of the political spectrum only aids those who would defeat the gay rights movement and keep gays in a position of social and legal subjection. Most people who harbor prejudice against homosexuals are not professional bigots like Dobson or Robertson; they are a rare class. On the contrary, most prejudiced people are not unintelligent or mean-spirited, but simply ill-informed and inexperienced. Because persuasive gay arguments are in disarray, or simply nonexistent, these countless ordinary Americans fall prey to the appealing lexicon of the professional bigots. An examination of that lexicon is crucial to understanding and refuting the antigay vanguard.

LIBERTICIDAL LEXICON . . .

First among the lexicon is the term "choice." Homosexuality is almost always cast by the antigay groups as a matter of choice. It is perhaps the most illogical of a host of misbegotten justifications. Why on earth, if one were really attracted to members of the opposite sex, would one choose to spend one's life marginalized and victimized, purely on a whim? It is also an uncommonly hateful argument, for it puts the onus on the victim—on every person who has ever been beaten up by gay bashers, bent by calls of "faggot" in the schoolyard, deprived of livelihood, or forced to live in desperation at the prospect of being "outed." It allows the perpetrators of such ugliness to distance themselves from the moral implications of their own actions and to blame those brutalized for the actions of the brute. Yet, for these very reasons, it is particularly effective. If people can be convinced that they are merely registering disapproval of a choice, they are much more likely to feel morally justified in disapproving of the immoral and, thereby, will vote for antigay laws, support antigay initiatives, and bend their efforts to curbing perverse volition.

For this reason, perhaps the chief question that must be confronted by gays today is whether homosexuality is a matter of choice? In 1920, British poet and novelist Vita Sackville-West wrote concerning homosexuality:

> I advance, therefore, the perfectly accepted theory that cases of dual personality do exist, in which the feminine and the masculine elements alternately preponderate. I advance this in an impersonal and scientific spirit, and claim that I am qualified to speak with the intimacy a professional scientist could acquire only after years of study and indirect information, because I have the object of study always at hand, in my own heart, and can gauge the exact truthfulness of what my own experience tells me. However frank, people would always keep something back. I can't keep back anything from myself.[25]

Here Sackville-West makes a key observation about homosexuality. She acknowledges the biology of the whole thing. It's "scientific," as she puts it, an uncontrollable product of nature. This, of course, is not a universally accepted view. "You choose to be gay, right?" is not an uncommon question for the gay individual to hear from curious acquaintances. Or perhaps one is asked, "Did you have an overbearing mother?" a quackery directly traceable to Sigmund Freud. People are more than ready to believe that homosexuality is somehow chosen or, if not completely volitional, at least nurtured and, therefore, capable of being consciously eschewed.

For the bigot, there is a certain measure of self-preservation in this embracing of ignorance. Homophobes justify their prejudice by casting it as a register of moral disapprobation for a chosen behavior. It is startling and unsettling when a gay person or a person who purports to be gay adopts this line of argument. For example, several years ago, I caught an episode of the *Montel Williams Show* on which Donna Minkowitz, a well-known gay activist, made an appearance. At the time, I didn't recognize the importance of Minkowitz's comments but I certainly never forgot them. Minkowitz brashly told Williams and his audience that she was fed up with the idea that the movement wouldn't increase the number of gays and lesbians in America. "There are more of us than there used to be," she intoned. She went on to validate practically every homophobic thing I've ever heard. She decried the idea that homosexuality is a product of nature, stating that the idea grew out of an oppressed group trying to put itself on par with its oppressors by asserting a common biological link. She then proudly proclaimed that she had *chosen* to be gay and that because of the gay movement more straight people would choose to be gay as well. She even agreed with Pat Robertson that gays were pitted in a war for the soul of America, implicitly agreeing that gays are intent on corrupting America's youth—Anita Bryant was, no doubt, pleased.

I remember my feelings of disgust at Minkowitz's performance, the ferocity of her militancy and her mean-spiritedness. Looking back, I'm not sure what upset me more—that Minkowitz said what she did (I am certainly not interested in battling for anyone's soul, that sort of thing can remain the mandate of Mr. Robertson)—or that the *Montel Williams Show* chose Minkowitz to *represent* the gay community. Certainly she is sensational, which I'm sure is all that the *Montel Williams Show* cared about, but even Minkowitz would admit that she is out of bounds for many of the most militant gay activists. I wonder what person, what stable, balanced person, would choose to be marginalized and to place herself into a group viewed as deviant and *unnatural*. I wonder why anyone who purports to advance gay rights would choose to paint homosexuality as something so awful and would choose to validate prejudices.

These prejudices, of course, still exist. Recently in Winston-Salem, North Carolina, the town in which I live, a local church hosted a therapist, a purported *reformed* lesbian, who theorized that being gay was a choice and that gays could be taught to be straight. Even though the self-proclaimed therapist freely admitted that she had no psychology or counseling credentials, the superintendent of the school system sent around an e-mail to his administrators encouraging them to attend. This should have surprised no one, because this is the same superintendent who objected to the inclusion of sexual orientation in the school system's antidiscrimination policy. Nevertheless, the local news media got wind of the goings on and had a field day. The administration justified itself by saying it merely had offered an alternative view.

Alternative, yes. Acceptable, no.

If Minkowitz and the visiting therapist chose to be gay, they are nothing more than masqueraders. They certainly are not now, nor have they ever been, homosexual. Any of us can choose to perform sexual acts with anyone else. That no more defines our sexual orientation than peroxide defines our hair color. The folly of such arguments is that they reduce being gay to its physical elements (it could also be argued that people like Minkowitz reduce it to a purely political thing, which is equally as shameful). Certainly the physicality is there, but the actual physical act is merely an expression of the true content of being gay. Being gay is to be, by nature, more attracted to a person of one's own sex than to a member of the opposite sex, and that attraction is a whole attraction, with every intimate, emotional, psychological, and, yes, sexual aspect that a straight relationship possesses.

But this reduction of everything gay to mere sex is a stereotype shared with other maligned groups. The hateful treatment of African American males in the Jim Crow South often was based upon the belief in the sexually diabolic Negro, who had to be lynched before he could defile another white woman. The Jew, too, has been imbued with unnatural sexual lust and perversion by the Nazis. These unfounded bigotries have been repeated with regard to homosexuals by the likes of Anita Bryant and the Save Our Children campaign or the Catholic Church, which pronounces homosexuals synonymous with pedophiles. To willfully perpetuate that bias in the way that Minkowitz and others have is unthinkable and hysteric.

People who talk about their sexual orientation in terms of choice are one of two things: (1) completely ignorant of their own sexuality; or (2) so caught up in their own self-empowerment that they have to think of their sexual orientation as a matter of taking control rather than as a surrender to the inevitable. Minkowitz is merely an example I was unfortunate enough to see on television. Similar rhetoric is prevalent in the gay subculture. I suppose to some it is appealing because it forcefully asserts differences first rather than having them spun by enemies later. It is also a way, by saying outlandish things, that people grab attention and headlines. For instance, I have encountered gay people who will loudly proclaim that they have no straight friends: "What could I possibly have in common with these less-evolved creatures?" they inquire. I don't think for a second that they actually believe this, but they say so because it is one more separatist element; it sets them apart, and it validates their feelings of martyrdom.

This is reflective of a major contributing factor to the slow pace of gay advancement in this country: From the beginning, the debate has been dominated by people who have nothing to say at all. People like Minkowitz seem to get all of the attention, because they are speaking louder and more absurdly than the rest of us. Gays who already feel marginalized latch onto the rhetoric because it gives them an identity to claim and a feeling of belonging. For people reaching out for a place to belong, rhetoric that makes homosexuality seem like an exclusive club rather than a biological function certainly has its appeal. This mind-set manifests itself in the extreme in the so-called bug chasers of the subculture—young people, usually men, who actively engage in reckless sexual behavior with the intention of contracting HIV. Their sense of displacement is so great that they seek actualization and belonging—belonging to anything—in the most horrific of ways.

All of this choice rhetoric now faces heavily mounting scientific evidence to the contrary. Studies linking homosexuality to biology are becoming numerous. Some of them, I must admit, have a greater ring of verity than others. Many of the studies are problematic because of limited replication, small samples, or both. What cannot be denied, at least by those who approach the question in good faith, is that evidence that sexual orientation is in some way biologically determined is increasing.

Some geneticists have theorized that being gay, at least among males, is determined by certain markers in the Xq28 chromosomal region. Skeptics, of course, argue that, if homosexuality is genetic and if homosexuals cannot procreate (at least if they live life as homosexuals), then these genes could not survive. This is not a totally invalid skepticism. There is much about homosexual genetics that we don't know; perhaps we don't know most of it. The scientific community suggests, rather, that it is not the existence of a particular "gay gene" that determines homosexuality, but rather a combination of genes that produces the homosexual. This evidence is persuasive. If homosexuality is genetically determined then one logically could expect twins to share sexual orientation. Studies show the likelihood that the identical twin of a gay person also will be gay to be about twice that of a fraternal twin of a gay person.

There is more to the biology argument than genetic loading. Some biologists suggest that homosexuality is corollary to brain anatomy. Gay men have larger suprachiasmatic nuclei, the part of the brain that affects (the magic word) behavior. Other studies show that most gay men have a larger isthmus of the corpus callosum, also a characteristic of left-handed people. Independent studies show that gays are 39 percent more likely to be left-handed than are straight people. Still other studies indicate that homosexuality is directly related to the level of androgens in the womb during gestation.

This emerging biology of homosexuality has serious implications for the continuation of antigay prejudice. I'm not suggesting that if homosexuality were concretely proven to be biologically determined, antigay discrimination suddenly would vanish. Heaven knows that the human race has a history of discrimination on the basis of biology. I have to look no further than my own country's antebellum past for proof.

But homosexuality as biological goes a long way toward debunking the "against nature" and religious arguments upon which antigay prejudice is founded. If homosexuality is imbedded in natural design, then it cannot, by definition, be unnatural. Excluding a person on the basis of biology is out of sync with the New Testament theology of the Christian right. Saint Paul's life, after all, was devoted to sharing what had begun as a gift for a select few, determined by their Jewish biology, with a great many, the rest of the human family.

Some years ago, I saw a production of the *Laramie Project,* the thespian chronicle of the death and aftermath of the death of a young college student, Matthew Shepard, in Wyoming. The aftermath, in my opinion, was pretty predictable. Liberals sighed and wrung their hands, and the Christian right, at its most magnanimous, loved the sinner but hated the sin that exacted his death and, at its worst, used Shepard's death as a foreshadowing of the horrific cosmic end destined for all gays on account of their transgression. But most saddening and nauseating was the statement of Wyoming Governor Jim Geringer who admonished gays not to "use Matt to further an agenda." Agenda is another familiar word in the antigay lexicon. But as Gore Vidal rejoined in the *Advocate,* "we must further [an agenda] if good is ever to come from the ooze and the slime where Matt's death came from."[26]

Indeed, our agenda must be to eradicate the incitatory notion that one chooses to be gay. We must convince a majority of Americans, we must impress upon them, the utter sadness and incomprehensibility that, in this, allegedly, the most generous nation on earth, a young man can be beaten and left to die lashed to a crude fence in rural Wyoming, all on account of a biological trait.

Even without the scientific information available, one needs only to look at the historical and current position of gays in this society to understand that sexual orientation is not a matter of choice. Who would choose to be marginalized, victimized, brutalized? Gays, until recently, faced jail terms for being gay; they continue to face dismissal from jobs, discrimination in housing, persecution from family and perceived friends, and pariah status in many religious faiths. In the face of these observations, the idea that homosexual orientation is a choice defies logic. Of course, any sexual expression entails some element of choice. One may have a sexual experience with whomever one chooses; a gay male has the physical capability to engage in sexual intercourse with either a male or female partner. But biology can complicate even this exercise of volition; sexual arousal is not subject to the exercise of the will. Moreover, one has considerably more difficulty, if it is possible at all, in choosing the person with whom one will form a romantic bond and ultimately fall in love. Being gay involves all of these things, just as being straight does. One can choose to repress one's self or even to marry a partner of the opposite sex and begin a family; but one can keep up such deception only for a finite period. Eventually, the true self emerges; there are countless broken families, families that began as a homosexual's effort at self-reform, that testify to that fact.

I don't need science to tell me the origin of my sexuality. Like Sackville-West before me, I have the object of study always at hand, in my own heart, and I can gauge the exact truthfulness of what my own experience tells me. But, for the sake of our quest for equality as a people, gays need science and the truth that comes from it. In my opinion, our position will not improve until society stops believing that gays deserve less than equal treatment because we have made less than prudent choices about our sexuality. Some gays genuinely fear that, if they support the biological argument, their kind eventually will be eliminated through genetic screening and the like. For the sake of our movement, however, we must put aside our fears and the junk psychology by which we have learned that our mothers, or a host of other factors, are to "blame" for our sexuality. We *must* embrace the integrity that legitimate science has to offer us.

The rhetoric of lifestyle and choice is something that must be battled with zeal and coherence. Gays must work, first, not to fall for the rhetoric themselves and, second, to point out its fallacies to the general public. Only when the lies underpinning discriminatory public policy are dispelled by the truth will those policies meet their demise.

THE FUTURE . . .

The natural culmination of this sort of institutional survey is to ask the question: How encouraging is the prospect for equality in the near future? After the decriminalization of homosexual sex by decree of the U.S. Supreme Court in *Lawrence v. Texas*, the natural progression is the legalization of marriage or its close equivalent for gay couples. Barring the enactment of some federal marriage amendment, only the U.S. Supreme Court is in a position to rid the nation of inequality in this sphere of human rights. This the high court could do by the mere stroke of a pen, but there is no indication that the Court is poised to take such action. One could optimistically believe that the Court's decision in *Lawrence*, or perhaps even its precedent beginning with *Romer v. Evans*, indicates the beginning of a trend that ultimately will bring the marriage question to a positive resolution.

Still, there are other forces to consider. The legislatures of many states as well as the federal Congress are at work on constitutional amendments that could prove to be insurmountable obstacles in the quest for gay marriage. Assuredly though, if allowed to last, the gay marriage experiment in Massachusetts should certainly allay fears and weaken the public's attachment to the hetero-dominated view of marriage.

Lawrence, whether or not the Court would so acknowledge, is testament to the proposition that the Court observes and often follows public opinion. As public opinion changed with regard to gay rights in the interval between *Bowers* and *Lawrence* so did the position of the Court. If states like Massachusetts and Vermont can teach the public the important lesson of equality that is explicit in the same-sex union experiments going forward there, it is likely that the lesson will not be lost on the Court. Progress is at work. I am reminded of Walter Benjamin's famous description of his prized possession, a work by Paul Klee, titled *Angelus Novus*. Benjamin writes:

[The painting] shows an angel looking as though he is about to move away from something he is fixedly contemplating. His eyes are staring, his mouth is open, his wings are spread. This is how one pictures the angel of history. His face is turned toward the past. Where we perceive a chain of events, he sees one single catastrophe which keeps piling wreckage upon wreckage and hurls it in front of his feet. The angel would like to stay, awaken the dead, and make whole what has been smashed. But a storm is blowing from Paradise; it has got caught in his wings with such violence that the angel can no longer close them. This storm irresistibly propels him into the future to which his back is turned, while the pile of debris before him grows skyward. This storm is what we call progress.[27]

I don't think it is too romantic to believe that a wind now stirs in Paradise; there is much reason to hope that we are witnessing the beginning of the end of second-class citizenship for gays, rather than witnessing the end of the beginning.

After all, if heterosociety fears a loss of its power by yielding to gay demands, this is merely an indication that heterosociety recognizes that it is confronted by a power in its own right. Power at bay is merely the residue of thoughts and habits that can yield and shift to include other, previously excluded groups. This inclusion, of course, necessarily means an end to the status quo. Consequently, there is resistance on the part of the powerful to recognizing, to owning, the hurt and pain—the price—exacted from those people upon whose deprivation their power depends. If the powerful cannot acknowledge this, they are left to imagine a reason why the marginalized, the powerless, are unhappily defiant. This defiance the powerful typically reduce to a rebellion against all civilization and civilized virtue. They are then haplessly convicted of measures, like the marriage amendment, which make up in absurdity, spitefulness, and unabashed cruelty what they lack in rationality and morality. But this cruelty does not prove that the powerful are resolute and never to be won over; rather, it demonstrates that they are desperate and that they perceive the energy that has them at bay. This should, on occasion, invest gays with a little patience, while exhorting that we can no longer neglect our important public duties. We must turn our attention to our communal existence in order for the gay rights cause to move forward.

The extreme emotional poles of the gay rights issue are starkly contradictory: the fire-and-brimstone pastor, like the Reverend Fred Phelps of Matthew Shepard infamy, resigning gays to hell from behind a fruitwood pulpit and the shrill cries of the ACT UP activist calling a Roman Catholic prelate a common murderer. Yet these polar opposites reflect the current American condition. During his aborted presidential campaign, John Edwards spoke of America as "two countries." During the media coverage of the 2004 election, we often heard our country spoken of as a "red" and a "blue" America, referring to the colors assigned on a map to the states that voted for George W. Bush and John Kerry, respectively. In the election aftermath, Jonathan Darman, associate editor for *Newsweek,* referred to the sharp division of the "two Americas" as a "mandate for culture war." The fundamentalist pastor and the ACT UP activist are the physical manifestations of the political polarization neatly summed up in these phrases.[28]

But we are not two countries, and, if gays are to attain equality, it will be in an America possessed of (or perhaps possessed by) both ideologies. How, the reader might question, are we ever to come to a resolution of such a divided national conscience? Here again, transformative politics, with its focus on equality and on national social evolution, offers the best hope. The focus must not be a posture of defense, but rather an attention to the opening up of previously unknown possibilities. Transformative politics is about more than regulation or power, although these are valid concerns; it is about securing public acceptance and achieving a de facto as well as a de jure equality. To be truly successful, gays must connect gay rights to the core of the American democratic tradition. Gay rights must become salient to people with no immediate stake in the culture wars. It must become relevant to them in the same way the abolition of slavery became relevant and important to individuals who were neither slaves nor slaveholders, relevant because they saw how it affected the fundamentals of the American tradition. Only when gays connect their goals to this sort of broader worldview will the landscape of gay rights be radically transformed for the better.

It is evident that the issues raised by gays and lesbians—intentionally or not—have become the subject of intense national debate. As illustrated by cases like *Romer v. Evans* and by the various marriage victories across the states and municipalities, the quest for gay rights is a multidimensional quest and many of the formidable obstacles and much of the important work have a locus in the individual states and localities—the counties, cities, towns, and villages. When the U.S. Supreme Court struck down the ban on the local gay rights protections at issue in *Romer,* Justice Scalia, in dissent, wrote that "[t]he Court has mistaken a Kulturkampf for a fit of spite."[29] The otherwise obtuse reasoning of Scalia's opinion aside, he, at least, recognized the true culture war status of the gay rights debate.

The gay rights controversy goes beyond issues of taxation, highway construction, or ballot counting; the gay rights struggle involves an enormous conflict of worldviews and a divergence of fundamental values. For those on both sides of the issue, more is at stake than a simple sex act. For gays and lesbians, organizing to secure equality—politically or legally—is an activity essential for survival. Our sexual orientation has been made unavoidably public, and we, in turn, must mobilize to transform the political landscape; otherwise abuse and dishonesty will continue to prevail. Moreover, because a plethora of divergent constituencies and interests are involved, transformative politics must be a politics of varying and wide-ranging tactics. There must be coalition building, political organization, and candidate endorsement and support, financial contribution and volunteerism, and lobbying, as well as demonstrations, marches, boycotts, vigils, and broadcast visibility. In the book *Private Lives, Public Conflicts*, the authors canvassed various American communities and recorded the antigay establishment using every one of these techniques. Gays must rise to the challenge. Ultimately, transformative politics, with its focus on equality and humanity, will prove victorious. With apologies to my hero, James Baldwin, "Everything now, we must assume, is in our hands; we have no right to assume otherwise. If we . . . who must, like lovers, insist on, or create, the consciousness of the others—do not falter in our duty now, we may be able, handful that we are, to . . . achieve our country, and change the history of the world." We must now dare everything, for we have everything to gain—or lose.[30]

CHAPTER 4

What Gay People Want

Equality, and I Will Be Free

I think the first duty of society is justice.

—Alexander Hamilton

IN THE WESTERN TRADITION OF POLITICAL THOUGHT, which ultimately wrought the American Revolution, there are really two freedoms, or, perhaps more properly put, two aspects of whole freedom. One of these freedoms is what Orlando Patterson has called personal freedom, that freedom which, "at its most elementary gives a person the sense that one, on the one hand, is not being coerced or restrained by another person in doing something desired and, on the other hand, the conviction that one can do as one pleases within the limits of another person's desire to do the same." This is the freedom at the heart of decisions like *Bowers v. Hardwick* and *Lawrence v. Texas*. This is the freedom to love and live as one chooses insofar as one does not harm others through that loving or living. But to stop there with this completely individual liberty is to fall short, to possess only a certain hobbled freedom. To be completely free, one also must be possessed of the complement, civic freedom, crisply described by Patterson as "the capacity of adult members of a community to participate in its life and governance."[1]

After *Lawrence*, critics might say gay Americans finally possess individual freedom: They are now free to love without fear of criminalization. "Why, then," these critics ask, "aren't they happy people?" The answer lies

precisely in the lack of this civic or political freedom. In addition to the freedom to love as they choose, gays want the same rights as other Americans to
have their loving relationships recognized and respected. They want to be free
from discrimination in employment for no better reason than the employer
not liking something as intrinsic and immutable as their gender or race—their
sexual orientation. Indeed, to the modern American, true personal freedom is
virtually inconceivable when not matched with civic freedom. Thus, despite
Patterson's care in articulating this bifurcated definition, freedom—total, irreducible freedom—is a combination of personal liberty and civic freedom.

Only with the possession of this whole freedom can there be true equality. This always has been the case. Finding themselves free of the shackles
of slavery, African Americans certainly did not feel free and equal at the
backs of buses, chased by Bull Connor's police dogs, or lynched for sidelong
glances at a white woman. They were not free, relegated as they were to a
fringe citizenship in which they were neither participatory nor respected.
My friend, Maya Angleou, writes of the African American experience in
her poem "Equality," from which I took the title of this chapter:

You declare you see me dimly
through a glass which will not shine,
though I stand before you boldly,
trim and rank and marking time.

You do own to hear me faintly
as a whisper out of range,
while my drums beat out the message
and the rhythms never change.

Equality, and I will be free.
Equality, and I will be free.

You announce my ways are wanton,
that I fly from man to man,
but if I'm just a shadow to you,
could you ever understand?

We have lived a painful history,
we know the shameful past,

but I keep on marching forward,
and you keep on coming last.

Equality, and I will be free.
Equality, and I will be free.

Take the blinders from your vision,
take the padding from your ears,
and confess you've heard me crying,
and admit you've seen my tears.

Hear the tempo so compelling,
hear the blood throb in my veins.
Yes, my drums are beating nightly,
and the rhythms never change.

Equality, and I will be free.
Equality, and I will be free.[2]

Likewise, gay Americans no longer want to be ignored, heard as a distant whisper. To use another literary allusion (Capote), they are no longer content to be the "other voices" from "other rooms." Instead, they want to be participating members of the democracy of their country. "Separate, but equal"—that is separate from the civic polity—"is inherently unequal," declared the U.S. Supreme Court in *Brown v. Board of Education*, the case that ended de jure racial segregation. In that statement is the essence of what gay people want: To be equal and to be included.

Some critics will, no doubt, disparage my comparison of African American equality with gay equality. Some will say that gays have had an easier road; they can "pass" and hide their sexual orientation when the going gets too rough. But this passing, while it may have saved a neck from the noose, is in no way less of a relinquishment of dignity, a loss of freedom, than otherwise inescapable victimization or brutality. Elementally, they are the same.

Equality, then, is the combination of personal and civic freedom; it is a combination of the private and the public. While it is fair to say that one cannot enjoy civic freedom without first possessing personal liberty, one is not free until one has a role in shaping the public mechanisms that govern one's destiny. As Michael Nava and Robert Dawidoff explain in their book, *Created Equal: Why Gay Rights Matter to America*, homosexuality is a public issue "because the heterosexual majority has elected to single it out as a characteristic for which an individual may be denied basic civic and human rights."[3] Sexuality has become a linchpin of citizenship. In North Carolina, the state supreme court has ruled that a parent's homosexuality can determine whether he will receive custody of his child. It is thus a foregone conclusion in my state that homosexuality, as a matter of law, has a negative impact upon children, even without demonstrable proof of harm. Our armed forces continue to be sexually segregated, and, in too many places in this country, gay people fear losing their jobs. They needn't be activists or squeaky wheels in the heterosexual machine to face these consequences; they need only be gay—even the most private, invisible gay person. Keeping your private life private is no guarantee you will be spared. Still, it is a Catch-22 for many gays; when one does make one's sexual orientation known, one's entire identity is recapitulated on that basis. Doors close; opportunities are often lost.

When I was a wisecracking teenager, I would tease my grandmother by intimating that she was shrinking with age, to which she would wryly retort, "I'm not shrinking, you've just hit your growth spurt." The gay community faces what might be referred to as the "shrinking homosexual" problem. Gays come out, only to find the informed world an inhospitable place. Unfortunately, they find little in the way of helpful support from the gay community. Too many gays are too concerned with keeping the private life private, failing to comprehend the inescapable public dimensions of their supposedly private selves. The gay rights movement lacks the cohesion of the other great civil rights struggles I have recounted: Equality is grasped at but never quite attained.

WHY SHOULD IT MATTER TO GAYS?

Why equality should matter to gay people, so evidently treated unequally, might to some seem like a silly inquiry. Yet it is an inquiry that merits addressing. I recently celebrated a birthday for which a group of friends gathered for a celebratory dinner. Among this group of seven were two men who dismayed me even more than had they been part of the gay right. These men were completely apathetic. The idea of discussing equality was, to them, unpalatable; as for the marriage question, they saw no reason—because they had no aspirations to marry—to bother with the issue. "It won't matter who's in office; no one will do anything for us. It's all empty rhetoric."

This attitude is all too pervasive in the gay community. There is, underlying our inability to make better progress in the quest for equality, a void of apathy, a vacuum sapping the life's blood from gay liberation. We have hidden our faces too long, satisfying ourselves with the empty rhetoric that, as long as we do not personally feel discrimination's lash, all is well—or is as good as possible. Yet all is not well, and we have the obligation to strive for better. Resting on tedious private security, we have paved the way for our continued disenfranchisement and worse. For every drag queen who threw a beer bottle in front of the Stonewall Inn, for every gay person who protested the acquittal of Harvey Milk's cold-blooded killer, for every thousand gay persons who marched in solidarity in the face of a politician's betrayal, there are millions more who have said and done nothing, all the while absorbing the blows to their dignity, complicit in their own inequality, hell bent on keeping their secret.

Gay men and women must realize and act on the truth that their homosexuality is not a personal problem but a thing of momentous political significance, which should be owned and treated as such. To these, the apathetic gays, I can put it no better than did James Baldwin: "This is your home, my friend, do not be driven from it; great men [and women] have done great things here, and will again, and we can make America what America must become."[4]

WHY SHOULD IT MATTER TO EVERYONE ELSE?

The humanity of every person is dependent upon recognizing the humanity of every other person. In a very real sense, those vicious people who struggle daily to perpetuate the subjugation of their fellow gay citizens can be seen to be victims of the very system they labor with such ferocity to maintain. The dehumanization of their brothers and sisters is ultimately their own dehumanization. The native people of South Africa have a concept I have 'written about elsewhere, the concept of *ubuntu*, which Desmond Tutu has described as an intertwining of humanity. *Ubuntu* cautions that, when any one of mankind suffers brutality, all of mankind suffers that brutality. The consequences of the practice of sexual apartheid in this country to those who enthusiastically support it are many. How easy it is when engaging in the dehumanization of another to accept the dehumanization of one's own self. How easy it is when decrying the value of any one life to forget the value of one's own life. People like Harvey Milk's killer are themselves dehumanized and brutalized by their victimization of others. Their descent into the muck and mire of oppression and hatred has turned them into beasts, unfeeling and incapable of understanding or compassion. Because our humanity is bound up in the humanity of *all* others, the consequences of contravening this law of nature are inescapable.

Likewise, in a society based on democratic values and the ultimate virtue of equality, as ours is purported to be, the diminution of the rights of any person or group is necessarily the diminution of the rights of all other members of the American polity. Refusing rights and fair treatment to the others, the minority, makes it all too easy for those rights to be wrested from us when we no longer find ourselves in the comfortable majority. Certainly, at some time in our communal history, we, or those like us, have been discriminated against because of a perceived difference; and, as certainly, the time will come again when we, or those like us, will be discriminated against on the basis of a perceived difference. The cycle must be broken.

If you are reading this as an apathetic straight, I challenge you: Take the time to get to know the gay people in your neighborhood, your workplace, your family—we are here. Confront your discomfort and the knowledge void head-on. Be careful to look beyond those opinions you may receive from closeted gays who might tell you that they do not suffer discrimination or that they are content and happy with the world in which they find themselves. They are not being truthful to you or to themselves. The things they say are colored by their confinement in the closet and, perhaps, by their fears of the world beyond the closet.

If you control or otherwise influence your office, your country club, your worship community, take a stand for what you must know, deep down, is right. Be a conscientious voter and understand the positions of those seeking public office. Make a commitment to humanity a paramount plank in every political platform.

Teach your children that prejudice and bigotry will not be tolerated; that it is a blow to their own humanity.

Love your gay children. Accept them. Understand them.

WHAT WE WANT . . .

Gay people want what all people want: acceptance and equal treatment. This is not the grudging tolerance currently accorded, but real unmitigated acceptance. We want more than the absence of brutality; we want to be able to pursue our own good in our own way; to define our own place and our own morality; and to pursue our own happiness, individually and collectively, without constant pressure to defend our right to do so. In short, we want freedom.

We want freedom from discrimination in employment; we want the freedom to serve our country by contributing to its armed forces while being open and honest about our sexual orientations. We want the freedom to love—sometimes to love and lose—within the same institutional framework as heterosexuals, imperfect as it may be. The freedom to marry is today the most contested issue concerning gay Americans; we want it contested no longer. Gays and lesbians want recognition of our full humanity, not merely as the sexualized creatures we have been made out to be at the hands of a zealous opposition. We want the lingering death of absurd suppositions about the superiority of straight parents to linger no longer. We want the laws our elected representatives make and the institutions our tax dollars support to be mindful—and respectful—of our dignity and our best interests. We want our private lives and our civic lives to be equal, in every respect, to the lives of straight people. We want the sexual barrier to a full and participating American citizenship removed. We want the measured beating of our drums to be heard—to be heard, and to be heeded: "Equality, and I will be free. Equality, and I will be free."

VISIBLE AND PARTICIPATING . . .

The only way gays can attain freedom and equality is by embracing transformative politics. We must become visible and participating members of the democratic society in which we live because it is inextricably intertwined with our private and public lives. Thus, I have attempted not only to outline the current situation of gays in America but also to illumine a path to equality and fuller citizenship. It can be summarized as follows:

1. Come Out

The importance of our visibility cannot be overstated. Except in extraordinary circumstances, every gay and lesbian person has, I venture to say, an affirmative moral duty to come out. Only when the majority of Americans knows and cares for a gay person can we realistically hope for large-scale change at every level where it is needed. Remaining in the closet is not your right; it is your burden, heaped upon you by a homophobic society that has made no place for you, no attempt to understand you.

Coming out does not mean shouting one's orientation from the rooftops to every person everywhere. It would be nice, of course, if our families and friends gave us unreserved support in every aspect of our struggle, but this is not always a realistic goal. Be true to your convictions, but exercise them wisely. There are many gays who live in circumstances in which revealing their orientation may endanger their lives, either the quality of that life or its very existence. Yet, you alone control your destinies. If you live under such medieval circumstances, take control of your lives—move or do whatever you have to do in order to liberate yourselves. Remaining in the closet is a perpetuated trauma, harmful to you, to other gays, to humanity. Your voiceless invisibility is more damaging than any maleficent act.

It may be difficult to imagine it now, but coming out will improve your life. Do not be tied to the tyranny of the culture that placed you in the closet, forever in fearful darkness; actively place yourself on the right side of history.

2. Understand and Combat Religious Bigotry

Do not underestimate the subversive, corruptive, bigoted agenda of the religious right. The damage they are doing to the American government cannot be overstated. Do not allow them to go unchecked. Expose their misconceptions and lies. Whether it is their intention or not, they are breeding hatred, creating violence and murder. They are poisoning America with a gospel of homophobia. Stop them!

Take your rightful place, if it is your choosing, as people of faith. Do not allow corrupt institutions to define your spirituality. Define your own relationship with your Creator and live it. Increase your own joy.

3. Practice a Responsible, Attentive Politics

Your gay sexuality has political dimensions beyond your control. Still, there is much about the politicization of your sexuality that you can control. We, as a community, are at a crucial point in American politics for which many courageous people have worked very hard. We have accomplished much, but we have much important work still to do. We must get beyond the damaging fallacy that tells us our privacy is the pinnacle of our struggle. Our equality is more than a matter of the famous "right to be let alone." The most important problem we now face is pervasive societal discrimination. We need more than a withdrawal of the state from our private lives; we need its active engagement in curbing the rampant discrimination against us.

In order to accomplish this we must acknowledge the public dimensions of our sexuality from which we often retreat. We must turn our attention to the too often neglected public, common institutions from which civic change is wrought. Only through an active, committed involvement in the American political process can we hope to secure the equality—the ultimate freedom—to which we are naturally, inherently entitled. We must turn our attention, our resources, and our talents to these important public matters so that future generations might celebrate their sexuality and increase their joy.

Equality, and *we* will be free.

EPILOGUE

Who Has Believed Our Report?

We are all citizens of history.

—Clifton Fadiman

T HIS BOOK HAS BEEN MY ATTEMPT to expostulate an effective gay politics. I have used the term politics here broadly to encompass not only
the American democratic process but also a democratic worldview. The two
are certainly not mutually exclusive. Indeed, I would venture to say that the
two can never really be separated if either is to be practiced and enjoyed
with any consistency. Politics can never truly be divorced from such considerations as religion, self-esteem, love, human emotion, or any of a host
of other factors that move our world and construct us as human beings. In
that way, the public and private gay self, at least in terms of the equality to
which we aspire, should not, and really cannot, be extricated.

On this tiny planet, there is not a hemisphere that does not crackle with
strife. Those born gay in this civilization, with the peculiar arrogance—as
Baldwin noted—to call itself simply *America*, have found here no exception
to that fact. They have been born into, in the words of gay pioneer Harry
Hay, a "subject-object culture," a male-dominated, heterocentric culture
that has been for them, on the whole, lethal.[1] For the most part, they have
hidden in the straight man's shadow, desperately trying to assimilate into
the straight man's world or, at least, to go unnoticed in it.

But in those early incandescent years of the homophile movement, gays
began to think of themselves not as the straight man's isolated aberration

but collectively as a group—different, yes—but independent of and equal in worth to the straight man. Weighed down too long by the repressive heterocentric stigma that is fairy, faggot, criminal, dyke, sodomite—homosexual—gays rebelled and began, for the first time, to construct their own identity. Their normalization was under way. Slowly, they transformed public opinion of themselves from perverse criminal to psychological patient to distinct sociopolitical minority.

Walt Whitman spoke of glimpsing reality through an intervening space in the quotidian madness of life—a glimpse of gay life set apart and unmolested by the whir of heterosociety rushing by.

> A glimpse through an interstice caught,
> Of a crowd of workmen and drivers in a bar-room around the
>   stove late of a winter night, and I unremark'd seated in a corner,
> Of a youth who loves me and whom I love, silently approaching
>   and seating himself near, that he may hold me by the hand,
> A long while amid the noises of coming and going, of drinking
>   and oath and smutty jest,
> There we two, content, happy in being together, speaking little,
>   perhaps not a word.[2]

In the early years of the homophile movement, gays seemed to have caught that glimpse too and, thus transfigured by it, were reluctant to let it go. A gay consciousness—the beginning of a gay politics—had emerged. Conscious, finally, that difference does not equal subhumanity, gays began to separate themselves from the country's recursive trap of heterocentric dominance and submission.

Over time, however, many gays have been lulled into the complacency of a false security. There is too much satisfaction in the mediocre, conditional acceptance society has thus far offered. Sometimes when I am lamenting the current state of things, a straight colleague of mine is fond of reminding me how far gay people have come in the last twenty years. He is, of course, correct; gay people have come far. Gays of my generation can scarcely imagine what it must have been like for those first recruits to the Mattachine Society in the early fifties. Perhaps that is the reason so many of the young are so inactive. Everywhere one looks it seems there can be found the clever imitator, persuading himself that things are fine as they are.

But things are not fine.

Several times in the preceding thoughts I have drawn examples from the African American civil rights movement. I will do so again here in these concluding words. In the afterword to the revised edition of *Virtually Normal*, Andrew Sullivan's thoughtful polemic on gay politics, Sullivan reminds us of a curious event in the liberal discourse about African American civil rights that turned consideration of that issue, at least in academic circles, on its head. This event was the 1959 publication, by the liberal opinion journal *Dissent*, of a provocative essay on race relations by Hannah Arendt.

The editors of *Dissent* were indignant over Arendt's wise paragraph, and almost didn't publish it. In the end, after a year's delay, they did publish it; but only accompanied by their own rebuttals excoriating it. What was the source of all this educated outrage? Quite simply, it was the genius of Arendt's classical liberal critique of the so-called liberal promotion of racial equality then taking place. Arendt chided the liberals for dealing with the outward reflections of racism before dealing with the central issues of basic humanity at racism's core. For example, Arendt saw the backwardness of addressing school desegregation while leaving antimiscegenation laws untouched. By pointing out the misguided, if well-intended, strategy of dealing with peripheral issues before conquering root causes, Arendt's short but incendiary critique touched off a firestorm, born as much, I suspect, from a frustrated realization of the verity of Arendt's argument as from anything else. Here is what she said:

The right to marry whomever one wishes is an elementary human right compared to which "the right to attend an integrated school, the right to sit where one pleases on a bus, the right to go into any hotel or recreation area or place of amusement, regardless of one's skin or color or race" are minor indeed. Even political rights, like the right to vote, and nearly all other rights enumerated in the Constitution, are secondary to the inalienable human rights to "life, liberty and the pursuit of happiness" proclaimed in the Declaration of Independence; and to this category the right to home and marriage unquestionably belongs.[3]

Like Arendt's work, and indeed that of Sullivan himself, the essence of this work has been the politics of human rights; its purpose has been to incite debate. Naturally, I would prefer this debate to be the proposition of as many people as possible, but if this work only redirects the discourse on the subject of gay politics for those already disposed to think about such things, as Arendt's did with racial discourse, I will feel my efforts vindicated. Foment of a dialogue, at whatever level, is critically important to gay rights.

Now, of course, Sullivan and I, perhaps even Arendt and I, diverge in reasoning on important suppositions about the ability to separate political and social equality. With the presupposition that political and social equality can exist independently of one another, I disagree; and that has been the argument of *Sexual Politics*. To hold the contrary position, one that would applaud adoption of antidiscrimination measures by a private employer, for example, but leave the government powerless to mandate identical provisions, is as irrational as it is ultimately futile. Indeed, there is precious little vindication in such measures when so many gay people still lack the basic human right to choose a spouse. The rapidity of change in the law of sexuality in this country is staggering; yet that cold fact remains.

Thus, marriage is important for the gay rights movement because it marks the moment when the most gays, as of yet, have crawled out of the shadow of their closely guarded privacy to assert their deservedness of the very public right to marry. Finally, the gay person's unfettered ability to proclaim his love in the most public and conventional way—marriage—will advance gay rights in a way that perhaps no other action can. Same-sex marriage may be an idea whose day has come, but I certainly will not live to see the day when a majority of American citizenry will be comfortable with gay marriage. Even this generation's children, I venture to say, will not see the day when most Americans are wholly comfortable with the concept. But children coming of age in the next generation will be the recipients of that privilege. They will see a day when no young gay man feels pressured into entering a heterosexual union when he does not naturally belong in one. They will see a world in which there is recognition that the stigma of homosexuality, not homosexuality itself, is the ultimate threat to the liberty Americans profess to prize.

This work has been my sincerest effort to answer the question to which I have distilled the Mattachine inquiries of a half century ago: "How shall we live?" The struggle to answer that question is, of course, the enterprise by which we ultimately illuminate our fellow humankind and come to an understanding of our commonalities and to a celebration of our differences. Because liberty is a thing grasped at but never finally attained—but also never finally lost—this struggle is the essential energy found in the dust of past civilizations and the animating force felt in new civilizations. Therefore, if I will not be granted the blessing of living in the world I so hopefully describe, it is my hope and my aim to join in the creation of such a blessing for future generations. That should be the aim of the gay rights movement. It is the only conceivable end for a truly principled sexual politics.

Appendix

The following are Web sites of many gay and nongay organizations working together to advance the rights of lesbian, gay, bisexual, and transgendered (LGBT) persons. Many of these Web sites can be accessed at the Freedom to Marry site, www.freedomtomarry.org, which has additional contact information and suggestions for getting involved.

NATIONAL ORGANIZATIONS

The Advocate

www.advocate.com/html/gaylinks/resources.asp
This is a well-known news and entertainment magazine with links to international LGBT related Web sites accessible from its resources page.

American Civil Liberties Union (ACLU)

www.aclu.org/issues/lgbt/index.html
The gay and lesbian rights page of the ACLU's Web site includes updates on the ACLU's efforts to advance gay rights, tracks LGBT issues in Congress, and provides access to informational electronic resources and newsletters.

American Psychological Association, Lesbian, Gay, and Bisexual Concerns Office

www.apa.org/pi/lgbc
Lesbian, Gay, and Bisexual Concerns Office at APA provides policy analy-

sis, supports APA policy development, and advocates APA policy on lesbian, gay, and bisexual concerns in psychology. It promotes psychological knowledge development and dissemination, provides technical assistance, information and referral, and consultation to APA members, other professionals, policy makers, the media, and the public. The site provides access to APA resources and amicus briefs filed by the APA in state and federal court cases.

American Veterans for Equal Rights, Inc. (AVER)

www.glbva.org
AVER, formerly known as Gay, Lesbian, and Bisexual Veterans of America, Inc., is a nonprofit chapter-based association of active, reserve, and veteran service members who support equal treatment and equal rights for members of the U.S. Armed Forces.

Children of Lesbians and Gays Everywhere (COLAGE)

www.colage.org
COLAGE is the only national and international organization specifically focused on supporting young people with LGBT parents. The site provides information on chapter activities and resources for advocates interested in lobbying on behalf of LGBT families.

Congress Online

www.congress.org
Provides information on representatives in your area as well as information on current legislation, bill status reports, and associations and advocacy groups that assemble rankings for representatives on issues of interest.

Couples National Network, Inc.

www.couples-national.org
Couples National Network, Inc., is a nonprofit organization that provides a social, educational, and humanitarian forum for gay and lesbian couples and promotes validity of same-sex relationships.

Dignity/USA

www.dignityusa.org
This is the largest and most progressive organization of LGBT Catholics in the United States and a proactive voice for reform in the church and in society. The site provides links to news articles about Dignity/USA activities, describes the structure of the organization, and includes contact information.

Don'tAmend.com

www.dontamend.com
This organization promotes an online grassroots campaign to prevent constitutional amendment banning gay marriage.

Family Pride Coalition

www.familypride.org
Family Pride seeks to advance the well-being of LGBT parents and their families. The site includes a list of family pride events, local parenting groups, links to books and articles, and links to other online resources.

Federal Web Locator

www.infoctr.edu/fwl
The Federal Web Locator is a service provided by the Center for Information Law and Policy. It offers links to the legislative, judicial, and executive branches of the federal government as well as to other federal agencies, corporations, and committees.

Firstgov: Your First Click to the U.S. Government

www.firstgov.gov
This site allows users to browse the U.S. government by topic and features a large database and index of all federal government Web pages.

Freedom to Marry Collaborative

www.geocities.com/evanwolfson
The Freedom to Marry Collaborative is a new organization working to win
the freedom to marry in at least one state within the next five years. The
site provides a list of resources and links to articles relevant to the fight for
marriage equality.

Gay and Lesbian Activists Alliance

www.glaa.org
The Gay and Lesbian Activists Alliance of Washington, D.C., is the
nation's oldest continuously active gay and lesbian civil rights organization.
It is a local, all-volunteer, nonpartisan, nonprofit political organization,
founded in 1971 to advance the equal rights of gay men and lesbians in
Washington, D.C.

Gay and Lesbian Advocates and Defenders (GLAD)

www.glad.org
GLAD is a legal rights organization dedicated to ending discrimination
based on sexual orientation, HIV status, and gender identity and expression. The GLAD Web site provides information on litigation, advocacy,
and educational efforts on behalf of LGBT individuals.

Gay & Lesbian Alliance Against Defamation (GLAAD)

www.glaad.org
The Gay & Lesbian Alliance Against Defamation (GLAAD) is dedicated
to promoting and ensuring fair, accurate, and inclusive representation of
gay people and events in the media as a means of eliminating homophobia
and discrimination based on gender identity and sexual orientation. Their
Web site provides more information about LGBT issues in the media and
resources for LGBT activism.

Gay and Lesbian Medical Association (GLMA)

www.glma.org
GLMA is a national organization committed to ensuring equality in health care for lesbian, gay, bisexual, and transgender individuals and health care professionals. GLMA achieves its goals by using medical expertise in professional education, public policy work, patient education and referrals, and the promotion of research.

Gay & Lesbian Victory Fund

www.victoryfund.org
The Gay & Lesbian Victory Fund is a national political organization that recruits, trains, and supports openly LGBT candidates and officials. The Web site allows users to search for public officials by state and includes information about candidates running for or currently holding public office.

Gay, Lesbian, and Straight Education Network (GLSEN)

www.glsen.org
GLSEN strives to assure that each member of every school community is valued and respected, regardless of sexual orientation. The site provides information for students interested in sexual orientation issues and describes how to get involved in student pride activities.

Gay Parent Magazine

www.gayparentmag.com
Provides information for LGBT individuals who are or who wish to be parents and provides gay-friendly resources for creating and nurturing different types of families.

Gender Education and Advocacy, Inc. (GEA)

www.gender.org
GEA is a national nonprofit organization focused on the needs, issues, and concerns of gender variant people. The site includes educational materials,

information on advocacy training, and technical assistance on behalf of transsexual and transgendered persons.

House of Representatives

www.house.gov
This site provides Internet addresses for home pages of the members of the House of Representatives.

Human Rights Campaign (HRC)

www.hrc.org
HRC is America's largest LGBT organization. The Web site offers information about renewing America's commitment to fighting HIV/AIDS, ending workplace discrimination, responding to antigay legislation, and focusing attention on LGBT health issues. The site includes information on LGBT-relevant legislation and talking points, and provides action alerts and sample letters that can be used to lobby Congress.

Immigration Equality

www.lgirtf.org
Immigration Equality is a national grassroots organization that works to end discrimination in U.S. immigration law against lesbian, gay, bisexual, transgender, and HIV-positive people, and to help obtain asylum for those persecuted in their home country based on their sexual orientation, transgender identity, or HIV-status. The Web site provides access to relevant resources including the *Status Report*, a newsletter that has up-to-date information on changes in immigration law.

International Gay and Lesbian Human Rights Commission (IGLHRC)

www.iglhrc.org
The mission of the International Gay and Lesbian Human Rights Commission is to secure the full enjoyment of the human rights of all people and communities subject to discrimination or abuse on the basis of sexual orientation or expression, gender identity or expression, and/or HIV status.

The Web site includes information about LGBT-related human rights abuses around the globe and provides a number of resources for those seeking asylum in the United States for issues related to sexual orientation.

Lambda Legal Defense & Education Fund

www.lambdalegal.org
Lambda Legal is a national organization committed to achieving full recognition of the civil rights of lesbians, gay men, bisexuals, transgender people, and those with HIV through impact litigation, education, and public policy work. The site provides information on current legal cases, special events around the country, and other LGBT resources.

Log Cabin Republicans (LCR)

www.logcabin.org
LCR is the largest national gay and lesbian Republican organization, with more than fifty chapters across the country. This site offers the opportunity to subscribe to a newsletter and to make donations. You can find local chapters as well as a listing of the board of directors, the National Advisory Board, and other personnel.

The Mautner Project for Lesbians with Cancer

www.mautnerproject.org
The Mautner Project is a national organization dedicated to lesbians with cancer, their partners, and caregivers. The site offers information on support and community services, and resources and referrals.

National Black Justice Coalition

www.nbjcoalition.org
The National Black Justice Coalition is a civil rights organization of black lesbian, gay, bisexual, and transgender people and their allies dedicated to fostering equality by fighting racism and homophobia. The coalition advocates for social justice by educating and mobilizing opinion leaders, including elected officials, clergy, and media, with a focus on black communities.

National Center for Lesbian Rights (NCLR)

www.nclrights.org
NCLR is a national legal resource center with a primary commitment to advancing the rights and safety of lesbians and their families through a program of litigation, public policy advocacy, free legal advice and counseling, and public education. In addition, NCLR provides representation and resources to gay men, and bisexual and transgender individuals on key issues that also significantly advance lesbian rights.

National Gay and Lesbian Task Force (The Task Force)

www.thetaskforce.org
The Task Force was the first national LGBT civil rights and advocacy organization. It serves as a national resource center for grassroots LGBT organizations at the state and local level. The site includes resources relevant to combating antigay violence, battling antigay legislative and ballot measures promoted by the radical right, advocating an end to job discrimination, working to repeal sodomy laws, demanding an effective governmental response to HIV, reforming the health care system and more.

National Gay Pilots Association (NGPA)

www.ngpa.org
NGPA is a national organization of gay and lesbian pilots and other aviation enthusiasts from across the country committed to creating an affirming social and professional network for gay and lesbian aviators, encouraging gays and lesbians to begin piloting careers, and fostering equal treatment of gay and lesbian aviators. The Web site provides listings of events and related links as well as information on scholarship opportunities.

National Latina/o Lesbian, Gay, Bisexual & Transgender Organization (LLEGO)

www.llego.org
LLEGO is the only national nonprofit organization devoted to representing Latina/o LGBT communities and addressing their growing needs regarding

an array of social issues ranging from civil rights and social justice to health and human services. The site provides information on upcoming events, programs for Latina/o LGBTs, and jobs within LLEGO's organization. It also provides links to relevant news articles as well as links to various resources for Latina/o LGBTs including youth, coming out, and mental health.

National Organization for Women (NOW)

www.now.org
NOW is the largest organization of feminist activists in the United States dedicated to bringing about equality for all women. Their Web site includes information on lesbian rights and equal marriage.

National Organization of Gay and Lesbian Scientists and Technical Professionals (NOGLSTP)

www.noglstp.org
NOGLSTP is a national nonprofit educational organization for LGBT people and their allies who are either employed in or interested in scientific or technological fields. The Web site provides access to selected articles from the *NOGLSTP Bulletin*; a list of members is available for networking purposes.

National Stonewall Democratic Federation

www.stonewalldemocrats.org
The federation provides information about mobilizing voters through a national grassroots network of gay and lesbian Democratic clubs. It works to advance gay and lesbian civil rights and supports nomination of Democratic candidates who support gay rights. It also educates voters on differences between the two political parties on LGBT issues.

National Youth Advocacy Coalition (NYAC)

www.nyacyouth.org
The NYAC advocates on behalf of LGBT and questioning youth. Through

their site, you can write elected officials, contact national and local media, read press releases, and find out about upcoming events. Their site has regularly updated information on legislative matters relevant to LGBT issues.

Parents, Families and Friends of Lesbians and Gays (PFLAG)

www.pflag.org
PFLAG acts to create a society that is healthy and respectful of human diversity. The site provides informational resources about equal rights, fostering dialogue about sexual orientation and gender identity, and other LGBT related issues.

Partners Task Force for Gay and Lesbian Couples

www.buddybuddy.com/toc.html
Partners Task Force focuses on issues of concern to same-sex couples, including legal marriage and support resources. The site has extensive information on alternative marriage, parenting, relationships, data, and links to other resources.

People for the American Way (PFAW)

www.pfaw.org
PFAW conducts research and supports legal and educational work. It also monitors the religious right movement and its political allies. This site provides vital information about civil rights issues for policymakers, scholars, and activists nationwide.

Pride at Work, AFL-CIO

www.prideatwork.org
Pride at Work is a constituency group of the AFL-CIO (American Federation of Labor and Congress of Industrial Organizations). Its purpose is to mobilize mutual support between the organized labor movement and the LGBT community around issues of social and economic justice.

Project Vote Smart

www.vote-smart.org
This Web site provides quick references to questions about government at various levels, including state, local, and city offices. It allows you to track the status of legislation and appropriation bills. The site includes information on broad government issues and provides links to current election information.

Proud Parenting

www.proudparenting.com
Formerly known as *Alternative Family Magazine*, *Proud Parenting* addresses the needs of LGBT parents and their families. On a state-by-state basis, the site provides links to resources on parenting groups, camps, reproduction, adoption and fostering, and national and international organizations.

Queer Day

www.queerday.com
Queer Day is an online magazine offering current news, articles, and reports, a discussion forum, and archives that you can browse by topic.

Queer Resources Directory (QRD)

www.qrd.org
QRD is an electronic library containing more than twenty thousand files about LGBT issues. Specific subjects can be searched by date or users may rely on general subject headings.

Servicemembers Legal Defense Network (SLDN)

www.sldn.org
SLDN is a legal aid, watchdog, and policy organization for service members harmed by "Don't Ask, Don't Tell." The site features a law library that includes relevant congressional testimony, court cases, Department of Defense memoranda and reports, executive orders, law journal articles, and various other useful resources.

SoulForce

www.soulforce.org
The purpose of SoulForce is freedom for lesbian, gay, bisexual, and transgender people from religious and political oppression through the practice
of relentless nonviolent resistance. The site includes information on upcoming events, support resources, and issues faced by LGBT individuals and
communities.

Stop the Hate

www.stop-the-hate.org
This organization is devoted to stopping hate crime. The site provides personal accounts of hate crime victims, resources for countering hate crime,
and informational links for those concerned with prejudice.

Teaching Tolerance

www.tolerance.org
Teaching Tolerance is a project of the Southern Poverty Law Center. It en-
courages people from all walks of life to "fight hate and promote tolerance."
The site provides informational materials for classroom use and a discussion
forum, and offers users a free magazine subscription.

Turn Out

www.turnleft.com/out
Turn Out features an extensive list of links to organizations and people involved in the political process and information specific to the LGBT community. The links provided are a good start for anyone researching LGBT
politics online.

United States Senate

www.senate.gov
Senate.gov provides a calendar of the day's activities for the Senate and allows users to search by number or keyword for information on bills and leg-

islative activities. The site also provides contact information for senators, including individual senators' home pages.

Universal Fellowship of Metropolitan Community Churches (MCC)

www.mccchurch.org
MCC plays a vital role in addressing the spiritual needs of the LGBT community around the world and seeks to provide an opportunity to explore a spiritual experience that affirms who we are. The site provides information on traditional and alternative understandings of Christian texts, a discussion forum, human rights news, and information on LGBT-relevant issues.

White House

www.whitehouse.gov
This site provides easy access to government information. It also provides insight into the president's policy perspectives and includes government reports relevant to high-profile legislation.

Whosoever

www.whosoever.org
Whosoever is an online magazine dedicated to the spiritual growth of LGBT Christians. The site includes articles, personal testimonies, and commentary on current topics.

ORGANIZATIONS BY STATE

California

California Freedom to Marry Coalition
www.civilmarriage.org

Equality California
www.eqca.org

Marriage Equality California
www.marriageequalityca.org

Colorado

Civil Rights Now
www.civilrightsnow.org
Civil Rights Now is a statewide, nonprofit organization dedicated to promoting community involvement in the LGBT family rights movement through education, coalition building, and mobilization. The Web site has information on civil marriage and parenting rights for LGBT families.

Connecticut

Love Makes a Family (LMF)
www.lmfct.org
LMF is a statewide coalition of organizations and individuals working for equal marriage rights for same-sex couples in Connecticut though community education, grassroots organizing, legislative advocacy, and lobbying.

Florida

Equality Florida
www.equalityflorida.org
Equality Florida is a statewide education and advocacy organization dedicated to eliminating discrimination based on sexual orientation, race, gender, and class. The organization brings together local advocacy groups, provides technical support, offers information and training on advocacy strategies, provides updates and interpretations on laws affecting the LGBT and supportive community, and responds to unfair or biased media coverage

Georgia

Georgia Equality
www.georgiaequality.org

Georgia Equality is the political advocacy voice of Georgia's lesbian, gay, bisexual, transgender citizens, and their allies.

Maryland

Equality Maryland
www.equalitymaryland.org
Equality Maryland works to secure and protect the rights of LGBT Marylanders by promoting legislative initiatives on the state, county, and municipal levels. The site provides information about their lobbying efforts as well as information about the activities of their sister organization, Equality Maryland Foundation, which works to eliminate prejudice and discrimination against LGBT Marylanders through outreach, education, research, community organizing, training, and coalition building.

Massachusetts

Freedom to Marry Coalition of Massachusetts
www.equalmarriage.org
The Freedom to Marry Coalition of Massachusetts engages in grassroots education, advocacy, and lobbying in support of civil marriage rights for same-sex couples.

MassEquality
www.massequality.org
MassEquality.org is a coalition of local and national groups dedicated to ensuring that the Massachusetts Supreme Judicial Court decision on marriage equality is upheld and that any antigay amendment or legislation is defeated.

Michigan

Triangle Foundation
www.tri.org
Triangle Foundation is an advocacy group for LGBT issues in Michigan public policy, religion, business, education, and bias-crime victim assistance.

Minnesota

Outfront Minnesota
www.outfront.org

Mississippi

Equality Mississippi
www.equalityms.org
Equality Mississippi is a statewide, nonpartisan, lobbying, education and
support network for LGBT communities in Mississippi. The Web site has
information about lobbying the state legislature, organizing communities,
and public education efforts.

New Hampshire

New Hampshire Freedom to Marry
www.nhftm.org

New York

Empire State Pride Agenda
www.prideagenda.org

The Wedding Party
www.theweddingparty.org

North Carolina

Equality North Carolina
www.equalitync.org

Southerners on New Ground (SONG)
www.southnewground.org

Oregon

Basic Rights Oregon
www.basicrights.org

Pennsylvania

Center for Lesbian and Gay Civil Rights
www.center4civilrights.org

South Carolina

South Carolina Gay and Lesbian Pride Movement
www.scglpm.org

Utah

Equality Utah
www.equalityutah.org

Vermont

Vermont Freedom to Marry Task Force
www.vtfreetomarry.org

Washington

Legal Marriage Alliance of Washington
www.lmaw.org

Wisconsin

Action Wisconsin
www.actionwisconsin.org

Notes

INTRODUCTION

1. Martin Luther King Jr., "Remaining Awake through a Great Revolution," sermon delivered at the National Cathedral, Washington, D.C., on March 31, 1968 in *A Knock at Midnight: Inspiration from the Great Sermons of Reverend Martin Luther King Jr.* (Warner Adult, 2005) (Audio CD).

CHAPTER 1

1. Clifford Krauss, "Canadian Leaders Agree to Propose Gay Marriage Law," *New York Times*, June 18, 2003.
2. *Lawrence v. Texas*, 539 U.S. 558 (2003).
3. Ruth Benedict, *Patterns of Culture* (New York: Mentor Books, 1946).
4. At this time, there was a general assumption that, along with insanity and mental retardation, sexual "perversion" was hereditary. Elimination of the ability to continue the spread of polluted traits was thought to be the most definitive way of halting the problem. See, e.g., G. E. Worthington, "Compulsory Sterilization Laws," *Journal of Social Hygiene* 11 (1925): 257–71; "Sterilization Bill: The Eugenics Society's First Draft," *Eugenics Review* 20 (1928): 166–68; Marie E. Kopp, "Surgical Treatment as Sex Crime Prevention Measure," *Journal of Law, Criminology, and Police Science* 28 (1937–38): 692–706.
5. N.Y. Penal Code, 1881 N.Y. Laws ch. 676.
6. William N. Eskridge Jr., *Gaylaw: Challenging the Apartheid of the Closet*, (Cambridge: Harvard University Press, 1999), 24.
7. Case law and statutory construction imported from England confined "sodomy" or "buggery" to anal penetration. But this crime was prosecutable between opposite-sex participants, even between husband and wife. *Rex v. Wiseman*, 92 Eng. Rep. 774 (K.B. 1718); *Regina v. Jellyman*, 173 Eng. Rep.

637 (1838). See also *Rex v. Jacobs*, 168 Eng. Rep. 830 (1817), holding that fellatio did not constitute sodomy.

8. Prior to 1900, only four fellatio cases went before the courts as criminalized sodomy. By 1920, however, twenty-four states had crafted laws that included fellatio in the sodomy definition.

9. A total of eleven states in the same year, 1920.

10. Mass. Gen. Laws. ch. 165, sec. 28 (1860).

11. The first cunnilingus conviction to stand was in a 1917 decision from North Dakota. *State v. Nelson*, 36 N.D. 564 (1917).

12. Arthur Lipkin, *Understanding Homosexuality, Changing Schools* (Boulder, Colorado: Westview Press, 1999), 78.

13. Model Penal Code, Tentative Draft No. 4 (Philadelphia: American Law Institute, 1955).

14. Michelangelo Signorile, *Queer in America: Sex, the Media, and the Closets of Power* (Madison: University of Wisconsin Press, 2003), xxi–xxii.

15. Ibid., xxi.

16. Christopher Isherwood, *A Single Man* (New York: Noonday Press, 1964), 72. Desmond Tutu, *God Has A Dream: A Vision of Hope for Our Time* (New York: Doubleday, 2004), 40.

17. Wendell Berry, *The Art of the Commonplace: The Agrarian Essays of Wendell Berry*, Norman Wirzba, ed. (Washington, D.C.: Shoemaker and Hoard, 2002), 8.

18. Barry Goldwater, "Ban on Gays is Senseless Attempt to Stall the Inevitable," *Washington Post*, June 10, 1993.

19. *U.S. v. Virginia*, 518 U.S. 571 (1996).

20. Barry Goldwater, "Ban on Gays is Senseless Attempt to Stall the Inevitable," *Washington Post*, June 10, 1993.

21. *U.S. v. Stanley*, 479 U.S. 1005 (1986).

22. Dana Blanton, "Majority Opposes Same-Sex Marriage," August 26, 2003, Fox News, http://www.foxnews.com/story/0,2933,95753,00.html (accessed March 3, 2006). Darren K. Carlson, "Public OK with Gays, Women in Military," December 23, 2003, the Gallup Poll, http://poll.gallup.com/content/default.aspx?ci=10240 (accessed March 3, 2006). The Gallup site is available to subscribers only.

23. Bruce Bawer, *A Place at the Table* (New York: Simon and Schuster, 1994), 239.

24. Ibid., 233.

25. Ibid., 235.

26. Joyce Murdoch and Deb Price, *Courting Justice: Gay Men and Lesbians v. the Supreme Court* (New York: Basic Books, 2001), 272, 335.

27. Alfred C. Kinsey, et al., *Sexual Behavior in the Human Male* (Philadelphia: W. B. Saunders, 1948); *Sexual Behavior in the Human Female* (Philadelphia: W. B. Saunders, 1953).

28. Richard Mohr, *Gays/Justice: A Study of Ethics, Society, and Law* (New York: Columbia University Press, 1988), 22.

29. Bruce Bawer, *A Place at the Table* (New York: Simon & Schuster, 1994), 243.

30. "Complete report on Gay Marriage," *Los Angeles Times*, April 11, 2004, http://www.latimes.com/news/nationworld/timespoll (accessed March 3, 2006).

31. Hutton Hayes, "Prison Camp," August 28, 2003, Advocate.com, www.advocate.com/html/stories/897/897_hayes.asp (accessed February 20, 2005).

32. Ralph Waldo Emerson, *Self-Reliance and Other Essays* (New York: Dover Publications, 1993), 19–38.

33. Dennis Altman, "What Price Gay Nationalism?" in *Gay Spirit: Myth and Meaning*, ed. Mark Thompson (New York: St. Martin's Press, 1987), 16.

CHAPTER 2

1. I had some reservation about what term to use in describing the religious phenomenon that animates so much of American political life. I, at first, was content with the term "fundamentalist," because it is the term with which we are most familiar when referring to religious groups who define themselves as "born-again" and who most often regard biblical scripture as the inerrant word of God. But, of course, in discussing the religious animus that animates homophobia, I had to deal with the Roman Catholic Church, which one does not normally consider fundamentalist, at least not by the criteria stated. I, therefore, decided to use the terminology "traditionalist" and "traditionalism" in an effort to be more inclusive of all the religious denominations operating in virtually the same way on the political scene. This compromise also left me unhappy because, in my view, most of the doctrinal positions I consider "fundamentalist" are not "traditional" in the sense that they do not reflect Christ's paramount commandment: "Love your neighbor as yourself." Consequently, I reverted to the fundamentalist/fundamentalism label. The reader must simply remember that, in the case of my argument here, it is the terminology most operative for dis-

cussion and that the Roman Catholic Church, for better or worse, is included.

2. In this essay, I adhere to convention and refer to God as "He," for no other reason than a desire not to check the reader's progress through surprise. Certainly, I do not believe that God is any specific gender; indeed, no measure of comfort or reverence would, for me, be lost (some might, in fact, be gained) had I shifted to the pronoun "She."

3. Richard Posner, *Sex and Reason* (Cambridge: Harvard University Press, 1992), 346.

4. Peter Gomes, "A Garden of Homophobia," *Advocate*, December 9, 1997.

5. Robert F. Nagel, "Playing Defense in Colorado," *First Things*, May 1998, 34–35.

6. Michael W. McConnell, "What Would It Mean to Have a 'First Amendment' for Sexual Orientation?" in *Sexual Orientation and Human Rights in American Religious Discourse*, ed. Saul M. Olyan and Martha C. Nussbaum (New York: Oxford University Press, 1998), 252.

7. Colorado Constitution, Article II, § 30b.

8. *Romer v. Evans*, 116 S. Ct. 1620, 1624 (1996).

9. Letha Scanzoni and Virginia Ramey Mollenkott, *Is the Homosexual My Neighbor?: A Positive Christian Response*, rev. ed. (New York: HarperCollins, 1994), 3.

10. In June 2005, the Canadian parliament passed a law recognizing same-sex marriage. The Spanish parliament also recognized gay marriage in June, 2005, making it the third European nation, along with the Netherlands (2000) and Belgium (2003), to do so.

11. Adolf Hitler, "Proclamation to the German Nation," radio address given Feb. 1, 1933, in *Hitler, Speeches and Proclamations 1932–45: The Chronicle of a Dictatorship*, ed. Max Domarus, vol. 1 (Wauconda, Ill.: Bolchazy-Carducci Publishers, 1990), 233. Doreen Brandt, "Jerry Falwell Forms Anti-Gay Marriage Coalition," 365.com Newscenter, http://www.365gay.com/NewsContent/080703falwellMarriage.htm (accessed February 17, 2006).

12. Jerry Falwell, "Founding Fathers-Liberty Alliance," August 10, 2000, http://www.mcbible.com/Misc Data/Founding Fathers.htm (accessed February 17, 2006).

13. James Dobson, "Was America a Christian Nation?," 1996, http://www.cs.umanitoba.ca/jacobn/jacobs/articles/dobson.html (accessed February 17, 2006). David Cantor, *The Religious Right: The Assault on Tolerance and Pluralism in America*, ed. Alan M. Schwartz (New York: Anti-Defamation

League, 1994). Michael Novak, *God's Country: Taking the Declaration Seriously* (Washington, D.C.: AEI Press, 2000), 16–17. Alan Dershowitz, *America Declares Independence* (Hoboken, New Jersey: John Wiley & Sons, 2003), 12. Alan Keyes, address to the Declaration Foundation, "Declaration Principles Reborn," August 11, 1996. John Ashcroft, "The Ashcroft File," American Atheists, http://www.atheists.org/action/ashcroftfile.html#bobjones (accessed February 17, 2006).

14. *Bowers v. Hardwick*, 478 U.S. 186 (1986) (Burger, C. J., concurring).

15. Ibid.

16. *Bowers v. Hardwick*, 478 U.S. 186 (1986) (Blackmun, J., dissenting).

17. David W. Moore, "Moral Values Important in the 2004 Exit Polls," December 7, 2004, the Gallup Poll, http://poll.gallup.com/content/default.aspx?ci=14275 (accessed March 3, 2006). The Gallup site is available to subscribers only.

18. Alasdair MacIntyre, *After Virtue: A Study in Moral Theory*, 2nd ed. (Notre Dame, Ind.: University of Notre Dame Press, 1984).

19. Pat Robertson, *700 Club* broadcast, July 2, 1996, quoted in Bruce Bawer, *Stealing Jesus: How Fundamentalism Betrays Christianity* (New York: Crown Publishing, 1997), 69.

20. Stephen Mitchell, *The Gospel According to Jesus* (New York: HarperCollins, 1993), 5.

21. Jefferson to Peter Carr, August 10, 1787, in *The Life and Selected Writings of Thomas Jefferson*, edited and with an introduction by Adrienne Koch and William Peden (New York: Modern Library, 1998), 397.

22. Thomas Paine, *The Age of Reason* (New York: Citadel, 1974), 157. Jefferson to John Adams, April 11, 1823, in Allen Jayne, *Jefferson's Declaration of Independence: Origins, Philosophy, and Theology* (Lexington: University of Kentucky Press, 1998), 34.

23. Allen Jayne, *Jefferson's Declaration of Independence: Origins, Philosophy, and Theology* (Lexington: University of Kentucky Press, 1998), 34.

24. Thomas Paine, *The Age of Reason* (New York: Citadel, 1974), 186. Thomas Jefferson, *The Jefferson Bible* (Boston: Beacon Press, 1989), 156.

25. Garry Wills, "The Day the Enlightenment Went Out," *New York Times*, November 4, 2004.

26. Letha Scanzoni and Virginia Ramey Mollenkott, *Is the Homosexual My Neighbor?: A Positive Christian Response*, rev. ed. (New York: HarperCollins, 1994), 60.

27. The Pope made the statement at a homily he gave in Central Park, New

York City, on October 7, 1995. It is archived at http://www.ewtn.com/library/papaldoc/jp2us95h.htm.

28. Eleanor Flexner, *Century of Struggle: The Woman's Rights Movement in the United States*, rev. ed. (Cambridge, Mass.: Belknap Press of Harvard University Press, 1975), 47.

29. Bruce Bawer, *Stealing Jesus* (New York: Crown Publishers, 1997), 253.

30. Laura Sessions Stepp, "Vatican Supports Bias Against Gays," *Washington Post,* July 17, 1992. Southern Baptist Convention Constitution, Article III: Membership, 1999–2005, http://www.sbc.net/aboutus/legal/constitution.asp (accessed February 17, 2006).

31. "San Francisco's Only Gay-Friendly Baptist Church Withdraws Its Application to the American Baptist Churches of the West," October 13, 1995, http://www.baptistchurchsf.org/aboutus.html (accessed February 17, 2006).

32. "Considerations Regarding Proposals to Give Legal Recognition to Unions between Homosexual Persons," July 31, 2003, http://www.vatican.va/roman_curia/congregations/cfaith/documents/rc_concfaithdoc_20030731_homosexual-unions_en.html (accessed February 17, 2006).

33. Garry Wills, *Why I Am a Catholic* (New York: Mariner, 2003), 6.

34. Bruce Bawer, *A Place at the Table* (New York: Simon and Schuster, 1994), 58.

CHAPTER 3

1. Gore Vidal, *Perpetual War for Perpetual Peace: How We Got to Be So Hated* (New York: Nation Books, 2002), 69.

2. 730 F.2d 444 (6th Cir. 1984).

3. Harald Ofstad, *Our Contempt for Weakness: Nazi Norms and Values—And Our Own* (Gothenburg: Almqvist & Wiksell, 1989), 275.

4. Desmond Tutu, *God Has a Dream: A Vision of Hope in Our Time* (New York: Doubleday, 2004), 40.

5. Martin Luther King Jr., *Why We Can't Wait* (New York: Harper & Row, 1964), 147–48.

6. Ibid., 149.

7. Felix Frankfurter, *Law and Politics: Occasional Papers of Felix Frankfurter, 1913–1938*, ed. Archibald Macleish and E. F. Prichard Jr. (New York: Harcourt Brace, 1939), 6.

8. David A. J. Richards, *Conscience and the Constitution: History, Theory and Law of the Reconstruction Amendments* (Princeton: Princeton University

Press, 1993), 75. Frederick Douglass, *The Frederick Douglass Papers,* vol. 2, *1847–54,* ed. John W. Blassingame (New Haven: Yale University Press, 1982), 385.

9. *Reed v. Reed,* 404 U.S. 71, 92 S. Ct. 251, 30 L. Ed. 2nd 255 (1971). *Reed* dealt with a statutory mandate that gave automatic preference to the father as the executor of a son's estate, over the mother, simply because the father was male. The Court held the state statutes unconstitutional.

10. St. Paul's admonitions in his first Epistle to Timothy (below), and others of his New Testament writings, were widely used in the South to justify the legality of slavery from a religious, moral standpoint.

    "Let as many servants as are under the yoke count their own masters worthy of all honour, that the name of God and his doctrine be not blasphemed. And they that have believing masters, let them not despise them, because they are brethren; but rather do them service, because they are faithful and beloved, partakers of the benefit. These things teach and exhort." 1 Tim. 6:1–3 Authorized Version (AV).

    "Let the woman learn in silence with all subjection. . . . I suffer not a woman to teach, nor to usurp authority over the man, but to be in silence." 1 Tim. 2:11–12 (AV).

11. Elizabeth Cady Stanton, Susan B. Anthony, and Mathilda Joslyn Gage, eds., *History of Woman Suffrage,* vol. 1 (New York: Fowler & Wells, 1881), 61, in Eleanor Flexner, *Century of Struggle: The Woman's Rights Movement in the United States,* rev. ed. (Cambridge: Belknap Press of Harvard University Press, 1975), 46.

12. William N. Eskridge Jr., *Gaylaw: Challenging the Apartheid of the Closet* (Cambridge: Harvard University Press, 1999), 82.

13. Melinda Henneberger, "Vatican Weighs Reaction to Accusations of Molesting by Clergy," *New York Times,* March 3, 2002.

14. A. W. Richard Sipe, *A Secret World: Sexuality and the Search for Celibacy* (New York: Brunner/Mazel Publishers, 1990), 71.

15. Garry Wills, *Papal Sin: Structures of Deceit* (New York: Doubleday, 2000), 194.

16. Ibid., 195, referring to surveys reported in James G. Wolf, ed., *Gay Priests* (San Francisco: Harper & Row, 1989), 60.

17. The beginning, I think, can be traced to Cardinal Ratzinger's (now Pope Benedict XVI) 1986 pronouncement on the sinfulness of all homosexual sex—which incidentally was the catalyst prompting John McNeill to defy the Vatican's ban on publishing *The Church and the Homosexual.*

18. George H. W. Bush, in an interview with ABC news reporter Stone Phillips, quoted in Bruce Bawer, *A Place at the Table* (New York: Simon and Schuster, 1994), 103.

19. S.J. 26, 108th Cong. (2003).

20. H.R. 56, 108th Cong. (2003).

21. 1 U.S.C. § 7 (1997).

22. House No. 3190 (Mass.).

23. When it became obvious that the amendment would fail in its second vote, opponents of same-sex marriage started a citizen's petition for a stricter amendment that would ban same-sex marriage without creating civil unions.

24. *Lawrence v. Texas*, 123 S. Ct. 2473 (2003).

25. Nigel Nicolson, *Portrait of a Marriage* (Chicago: University of Chicago Press, 1973), 106.

26. "J'accuse!" *Advocate*, November 24, 1998.

27. Michael W. Jennings, ed., *Walter Benjamin: Selected Writings*, vol. 4, *1938–1940* (Cambridge: Belknap Press of Harvard University Press, 2003), 392.

28. Senator John Edwards, "Two Americas" (speech, Des Moines, Iowa, December 29, 2003). A transcript is available at http://www.mintruth.com/wiki/index.php?Two Americas (accessed March 1, 2006). Mr. Darman's comments were noted by the author during a television broadcast covering the 2004 presidential election, on which Mr. Darman was a panelist.

29. *Romer v. Evans*, 517 U.S. 620 (1996) (Scalia, J., dissenting).

30. James Baldwin, *The Fire Next Time* (New York: Vintage Books, 1993), 105.

CHAPTER 4

1. Orlando Patterson, *Freedom*, vol. 1, *Freedom in the Making of Western Culture* (New York: Basic Books, 1991), 3–4, quoted in Elizabeth Fox-Genovese, "Contested Meanings: Women and the Problem of Freedom in the Mid-Nineteenth-Century United States," in *Historical Change and Human Rights: The Oxford Amnesty Lectures 1994*, ed. Olwen Hufton (New York: Basic Books, 1995), 180–81.

2. "Equality," copyright 1990 by Maya Angelou, from *I Shall Not Be Moved* by Maya Angelou. Used by permission of Random House, Inc.

3. Michael Nava and David Dawidoff, *Created Equal: Why Gay Rights Matter to America* (New York: St. Martin's Press, 1994), 60.
4. James Baldwin, *The Fire Next Time* (New York: Vintage Books, 1993), 10.

EPILOGUE

1. Harry Hay, "A Separate People Whose Time Has Come," in *Gay Spirit: Myth and Meaning,* ed. Mark Thompson (New York: St. Martin's Press, 1987), 289.
2. Walt Whitman, "A Glimpse," *Leaves of Grass* (New York: Vintage Books, 1992), 283.
3. Hannah Arendt, "Reflections on Little Rock," *Dissent* 6, no. 1 (Winter 1959).

Selected Bibliography

The following are works cited in the text, or helped to inform its argument:

Adam, Barry D. *The Rise of a Gay and Lesbian Movement*. Boston: Twayne, 1987.

Ball, Carlos A. *The Morality of Gay Rights: An Exploration in Political Philosophy*. New York: Routledge, 2003.

Bawer, Bruce. *A Place at the Table*. New York: Simon and Schuster, 1994.

————. *Stealing Jesus*. New York: Three Rivers Press, 1997.

Beemyn, Brett, ed. *Creating a Place for Ourselves: Lesbian, Gay, and Bisexual Community Histories*. New York: Routledge, 1997.

Blasius, Mark. *Gay and Lesbian Politics: Sexuality and the Emergence of a New Ethic*. Philadelphia: Temple University Press, 1994.

Boswell, John. *Christianity, Social Tolerance, and Homosexuality: Gay People in Western Europe from the Beginning of the Christian Era to the Fourteenth Century*. Chicago: University of Chicago Press, 1981.

Button, James, W., et. al. *Private Lives, Public Conflicts: Battles Over Gay Rights in American Communities*. Washington, D.C.: CQ Press, 1997.

Cain, Patricia A. *Rainbow Rights: The Role of Lawyers and Courts in the Lesbian and Gay Civil Rights Movement*. Boulder: Westview Press, 2000.

Chauncey, George. *Gay New York: Gender, Urban Culture, and the Making of the Gay Male World 1890–1940*. New York: Basic Books, 1994.

Dershowitz, Alan. *America Declares Independence*. Hoboken, N.J.: John Wiley & Sons, 2003.

Duberman, Martin Bauml, et. al., *Hidden From History: Reclaiming the Gay and Lesbian Past*. New York: New American Library, 1989.

Escoffier, Jeffrey. *American Homo: Community and Perversity*. Berkeley: University of California Press, 1998.

Eskridge, William N., Jr. *Equality Practice: Civil Unions and the Future of Gay Rights*. New York: Routledge, 2002.

————. *Gaylaw: Challenging the Apartheid of the Closet*. Cambridge: Harvard University Press, 1999.

Gerstman, Evan. *Same-Sex Marriage and the Constitution*. Cambridge, U.K.: Cambridge University Press, 2004.

Gilreath, Shannon. "The Technicolor Constitution: Popular Constitutionalism, Ethical Norms, and Legal Pedagogy." *Texas Journal on Civil Liberties and Civil Rights* 9 (Spring 1990): 23–44.

Hufton, Olwen, ed. *Historical Change & Human Rights: The Oxford Amnesty Lectures 1994*. New York: Basic Books, 1995.

Katz, Jonathan. *Gay American History: Lesbians and Gay Men in the U.S.A.* New York: Harper Colophon, 1985.

King, Martin Luther, Jr. *Where Do We Go from Here: Chaos or Community?* New York: Harper & Row, 1967.

————. *Why We Can't Wait*. New York: Harper & Row, 1964.

Lipkin, Arthur. *Understanding Homosexuality, Changing Schools*. New York: Westview, 1999.

McConnell, Michael W., et al., eds. *Christian Perspectives on Legal Thought*. New Haven: Yale University Press, 2001.

McNeill, John J. *The Church and the Homosexual*. 4th ed. Boston: Beacon Press, 1993.

Mitchell, Stephen. *The Gospel According to Jesus*. New York: HarperCollins, 1993.

Mohr, Richard D. *Gay Ideas: Outing and Other Controversies*. Boston: Beacon Press, 1992.

————. *Gays/Justice: A Study of Ethics, Society, and Law*. New York: Columbia University Press, 1988.

Murray, Stephen O. *American Gay*. Chicago: University of Chicago Press, 1996.

Nagel, Robert F. "Playing Defense in Colorado." *First Things*. May 1998.

Olyan, Saul M., and Martha C. Nussbaum, eds. *Sexual Orientation & Human Rights in American Religious Discourse*. New York: Oxford University Press, 1998.

Patterson, Orlando, *Freedom, vol. 1: Freedom in the Making of Western Culture*. New York: Basic Books, 1991.

Perry, Michael J. *We the People: The Fourteenth Amendment and the Supreme Court*. Oxford: Oxford University Press, 1999.

Posner, Richard A. *Sex and Reason*. Cambridge: Harvard University Press, 1994.

Richards, David A. J. *Women, Gays, and the Constitution: The Grounds for Feminism and Gay Rights in Culture and Law*. Chicago: University of Chicago Press, 1998.

Scanzoni, Letha Dawson, and Virginia Ramey Mollenkott. *Is the Homosexual My Neighbor?* San Francisco: Harper San Francisco, 1994.

Schulman, Sarah. *My American History*. New York: Routledge, 1994.

Sedgwick, Eve Kosofsky. *Epistemology of the Closet*. Berkeley: University of California Press, 1990.

Seidman, Steven. *Beyond the Closet: The Transformation of Gay and Lesbian Life*. New York: Routledge, 2002.

Signorile, Michelangelo. *Queer in America: Sex, the Media, and the Closets of Power*. 3rd ed. Madison: University of Wisconsin Press, 2003.

Sullivan, Andrew. *Virtually Normal: An Argument about Homosexuality*. New York: Alfred A. Knopf, 1995.

Thompson, Mark, ed. *Gay Spirit: Myth and Meaning*. New York: St. Martin's Press, 1987.

Tutu, Desmond. *God Has a Dream: A Vision of Hope for Our Time*. New York: Doubleday, 2004.

Vidal, Gore. *Sexually Speaking: Collected Sex Writings*. San Francisco: Cleis Press, 1999.

Wills, Garry. *Papal Sin*. New York: Doubleday, 2000.

———. *Why I Am a Catholic*. New York: Mariner, 2003.

Wolfe, Alan. *Moral Freedom: The Search for Virtue in a World of Choice*. New York: W. W. Norton, 2001.

Wolfson, Evan. *Why Marriage Matters: America, Equality, and Gay People's Right to Marry*. New York: Simon and Schuster, 2004.

Index